A Distinct and Separate Settlement

Governing Norfolk Island

DON WRIGHT

Copyright © Donald Wright 2026
First published by Hembury Books in 2026
hemburybooks.com.au
info@hemburybooks.com

Paperback ISBN 9781923517226
Ebook ISBN 9781923517189

The moral right of the author has been asserted.
All rights reserved. Apart from any fair dealing for the purposes of private study, education or research, no part may be reproduced, stored in a retrieval system, or transmitted, in any form or by any means, electronic, mechanical, photocopying, recording or otherwise, without the written permission of the author.

A catalogue record for this book is available from the National Library of Australia

CONTENTS

Preface 4
Chapter 1: Annie and the Empire 6
Chapter 2: Pitcairn Island 34
Chapter 3: Norfolk Island 63
Chapter 4: Hope and Disappointment 1914-1939 98
Chapter 5: World War II and Post-War Reconstruction .. 144
Chapter 6: Nimmo and After 209
Chapter 7: A Measure of Self-Government? 236

Select Bibliography 249
Abbreviations 254
End Notes 255
Acknowledgements 271
Index 272
About the Author 292

PREFACE

Norfolk Island is small, isolated and remote. Nevertheless, it has generated a large literature by and about its inhabitants. Why should this be? Its links with the descendants of the *Bounty* mutineers is one reason. Its natural beauty is another. But I think the main reason driving their deep involvement and engagement in public affairs is because of the ongoing debate about the extent to which the islanders are able to run their own affairs.

This work commences with the occupation of Pitcairn Island by the *Bounty* mutineers and their Tahitian consorts. We then shift to Norfolk Island in 1856, where they found that the expectations which they had when relocating from Pitcairn to Norfolk were not readily able to be fulfilled.

Norfolk Island is a place where political crises are common. Since 1856 the Island has endured several Royal Commissions, litigation in the High Court of Australia, and variations of the apparatus of government springing from, at one extreme, Councils with solely an advisory function, and at the other extreme a legislative assembly with a substantial degree of autonomy. At the moment the Island labours under an unclear fate. Partial self-government was removed in recent years, and the debate continues on.

This book is an attempt to obtain an understanding of what happened, and why, during the time before self-government, and afterwards.

Don Wright
Sydney

Chapter 1

Annie and the Empire

In August 1893, Annie Charlotte Greena Wiseman Christian lived with her parents in Quality Row, Norfolk Island. She was sixteen years old. Unmarried, she was regarded as "certainly not in the full possession of all her faculties". This she knew, though: that her pregnancy violated God's law and her community's view of propriety. So when, on the night of 25 August, Annie gave birth in her bedroom to a daughter, her next act had a sense of purpose that was explicable. She left the room with her infant, crossed the adjacent verandah, and put her baby down a well in the garden.[1]

Her pregnancy was (she believed) "undiscovered". Likewise, at first, the death of her baby. But her grasp of what she understood to be the expectations which surrounded her was not equalled by her subtlety of concealment. For the pregnancy was indeed known to her mother and other close relatives, and what she had done was soon uncovered. Her mother and aunt, who well knew of Annie's pregnancy although she herself denied it, saw the girl in bed, blood smears on the verandah and bloody clothing in her room. They went to Dr Metcalfe and told him of their suspicions. Metcalfe hurried to the house. He spoke to the girl, and examined her.

> After the examination, I charged her with having had a child, and asked her what she had done with it. She replied that she had had a miscarriage, but subsequently she admitted that she had given birth to a baby in the night, but that it was dead, and that she had thrown it into an old, disused well not far away . . . Immediately afterwards I rode to the Chief Magistrate's house and informed him of all the particulars I was in possession of. The Chief Magistrate at once proceeded with one of his councillors and several policemen, and, accompanied by myself, to the well, and at the bottom of it we could see distinctly the naked body of an infant; Mr G Adams descended, and placing it in a basket it was brought up and placed in my hands.

Metcalfe conducted a post-mortem examination and concluded that the child was alive when thrown into the well – a conclusion Annie denied, being sufficiently aware of her position when questioned later that day by the chief magistrate.

> "Have you been in the family way?" "Yes." "Have you the child – is it born?" "Yes." "When?" "About 2am today." "What did you do with it?" "Put it in a disused well by the cottage." "Was the child alive when born?" "It squeaked one time." "Did you feel it move before it was born?" "Yes." "Did it make a noise when you were going to the well?" "No." "Had you a light when it was born?" "I catch one match." "Did you see it living?" "I take it up – can't move." "How high when the baby fell on the floor?"

"Half standing." "Did you catch it?" "No." "Did you block the baby's mouth?" "No." "What did you carry it over in?" "An old skirt." "Were you sure the baby was dead when you threw it down the well?" "Yes."

The written depositions were sent to the governor in Sydney. The gravity of the offence was recognised as being beyond the jurisdiction of the chief magistrate, and the matter would have to be dealt with by the governor. But not without the chief magistrate's mitigation.

> The woman, in the agony of that dreadful night, alone in a darkened room, suffering the pangs of labour, with no-one to cheer or help her in the slightest, in her terror and shame could not have been conscious of what she was doing. . . . your Excellency holds the scales of justice. May I ask for a merciful consideration of this poor woman's case?

. . . .

Mercy though was not to be the first – or a principal – consideration. Annie Christian's case drew together a skein of beliefs and attitudes. Was not Norfolk Island settled, as a mark of the sovereign's favour, by the renowned and God-fearing Pitcairners in order to form a sort of autonomous theocracy, lapped in goodness by the fastnesses of the South Seas? Had this community so far fallen that infanticide was not only practised, but even gave rise to eloquent sympathy from those charged locally with the responsibility of upholding the law, both secular and divine? After all, as Metcalfe darkly hinted in a confidential letter to the governor in Sydney:

> I have reason to believe, though cannot prove, and therefore cannot officially report to Your Excellency, that criminal abortion has been more than once practised here during late years.

A community of fabulous religiosity, guiding itself by precepts analogous to those espoused by the Queen Empress herself, might well be permitted to dwell alone and apart from the apparatus of Empire. But did not the Empire have a duty to raise up those, whether in upper Canada, on the Nile or among the "Blacks of the wild Australian interior" who were "socially and morally in a very low condition" – even if the benighted, as in Norfolk Island, had previously been known for their adherence to the word of the Lord? The circumstances "I fear at present reflect little credit on our administration".[2]

Moreover, businessmen "complain that they have no means of recovering debts", thus infringing another tenet of the evangelical world view. The complaint was not new.

> From all accounts the people were degenerating into vicious habits . . . it is also affirmed that there is virtually no law . . . It has often been suggested that a stipendiary magistrate should be appointed, who would visit the Island periodically.[3]

Thus the governor, some seven months before Annie Christian drew the threads together. But how could the special dispensation for the Pitcairners be revoked? What means existed for the shepherd to bring the flock within the fold? Had the work of Sir William Denison and like-minded others, who fetched Pitcairners to the new Eden, proved too well-wrought readily to be undone? After all:

> The habits and modes of thought of the Islanders are so different from those of Englishmen; the circumstances of the colony are so unique, that I confess I should be sorry to see the laws of England or of New South Wales, either civil or criminal, adopted in the aggregate as the Laws of Norfolk Island.[4]

Were those views, re-expressed by Denison in 1859, to prevail? Certainly, practical obstacles abounded to any proposal to deal summarily with the *fin de siècle* decadence of the remote Islanders. The governor found this out when he attempted to respond to Annie Christian's despiteful usage of what was moral, lawful, and proper to believe.

The island's chief magistrate, Stephen Christian, had asserted that His Excellency "holds the scales of justice". His Excellency was unsure; the case had caused him "much perplexity" and seemed to "illustrate the unsatisfactory state of the law, and the difficulty of administering it under existing conditions".[5]

Intending rectification, the governor wrote to the attorney-general of New South Wales, Edmund Barton, in October 1893:

> The jury unanimously found the accused guilty of infanticide. I think the evidence supports their conclusion. The attitude of

the girl, as mentioned in Dr Metcalfe's private letter, as having "repented and being quite free from sin", would seem to make it necessary, in the interests of order and morality, that the gravity of the offence should be marked by a sentence, which would dispel the illusions which, according to Dr Metcalfe, seem to prevail. Should be glad of the Attorney-General's opinion:

(1) As to whether he concurs with me in thinking the jury justified in their finding.

(2) If so, what term of imprisonment under the circumstances would be an adequate punishment.

(3) As to my power of deportation, and confining the accused in a prison in this colony. I ask the question as I understand there is no proper prison in Norfolk Island.[6]

The perplexity was not to be relieved. Barton agreed that the evidence fully sustained the jury's verdict – "any other verdict would have been more merciful than moral."[7] But that verdict was no foundation for punishing the woman, who "remains unscathed unless tried and convicted by due legal process". Here was the rub. What was the legal process? What collision was to occur between on the one hand the desire for rectification, morality, order, and on the other the genesis of this peculiar island polity?

Barton set out the history. The inhabitants of Pitcairn Island, the descendants of the *Bounty* mutineers, were at their own request transferred by the imperial government to the larger and more productive Norfolk Island. By royal Order in Council of 24 June 1856, Norfolk Island was, in pursuance of statutory authority, "severed from the Colony of Tasmania to which it had stood annexed for some 12 years", and was constituted "a distinct and separate settlement". It was ordered that the affairs of the island were to be administered by a governor appointed for that purpose and the person holding the governorship of New South Wales was constituted and appointed for the like time Governor of Norfolk Island. Among his powers as such was the authority to appoint judges, justices of the peace, and other necessary officers and magistrates for the administration of justice in the island, and the making of laws for the order, peace, and good government thereof:

> It will be seen that the Governor of Norfolk Island has invested in himself as full and complete powers of legislation, subject only to the Royal Instructions, as are wielded by the Parliament of this or any other self-governing colony.

As for the royal instructions, the Governor of Norfolk Island was instructed to observe, as nearly as circumstances would admit, the royal instructions directed to him in his other capacity as Governor of New South Wales. Subject to this, however, he was:

> as far as might be consistent with this Regulation, and as far as practicable, to preserve the laws and usages by which the inhabitants of the Island had been accustomed to govern themselves in Pitcairn's Island; and . . . to adapt his authority under the Order in Council to the preservation and maintenance of such laws and usages.

The problem was, "due legal process" had not been followed. And it could not be followed until a properly constituted court was sent to the island. That would require funds, and funds were not forthcoming from the imperial authorities. Eight months later, in June 1894, the governor complained to the secretary of state that the case:

> has caused me considerable embarrassment. On hearing from Your Lordship that the Imperial government were not prepared to make any contribution towards carrying out the administration of justice in the Island, I had to reconsider the situation . . .[8]

The governor had previously, in December 1893, written to the secretary of state about immorality, and about money.

> Since my assumption of office, reports of a most unsatisfactory nature have reached me concerning the condition of Norfolk Island. These reports have come from the Chief Magistrate, his secretary, who I have seen, the Chaplain, and the Medical Officer; also from one of the missionaries, who has written to me on the subject. I have also had interviews with the Master of the vessel which trades between here and the island, and which is subsidised to carry the mail. From these sources of information, as well as from letters from businessmen, who complain that they have no means of recovering debts, I am forced to the conclusion that the island is socially and morally in a very low condition.
>
> The active functions of Government are in the hands of the

Chief Magistrate, who receives a remuneration of £25 a year, and who is elected by the people. The population, from their origin and circumstances, are all connected and intermarried, consequently any magistrate appointed by them is hampered by conditions of kinship and family interest. But even if it were possible under these conditions to obtain an impartial and competent magistrate, he has no means of enforcing the law, as there are no prisons on the Island, and the cases which he, assisted by a jury, can deal with are limited to minor offences.

Illustrating the difficulty in dealing with cases of serious crime, I forward in a separate despatch the details of the case of infanticide [Annie Christian's case], respecting which I am still waiting for instructions from your Lordship.

The laws and regulations at present in force, although they have been subject to some amendments, are practically the same as those established by Sir John Young in 1862 when the population was less than one-third of its present number. It appears to me that the community, confined as it is to a limited area, has entirely outgrown the circumstances and conditions under which these laws and regulations were established.[9]

The governor proposed that a commission of inquiry be sent to the island; that the possibility of appointing either a permanent resident or a visiting magistrate be explored; and that the establishment of a prison be investigated. Imperial funds were sought, though the raising of local revenue was not overlooked.

It has occurred to me, as a beginning, a small duty should be put on spirits and tobacco.

The private reply from Mr Meade of the Colonial Office was discouraging.

It is useless to go again to the Treasury about any financial assistance. Every possible penny is now being saved owing to the terrible financial returns which foreshadow an enormous deficit.

Do you think it possible that New South Wales could be induced to take over the island?

It was proposed about 6 years ago and the Colonial Government then feared that it would be impossible.

... They were at first favourable to the suggestion, but seemed to have altered their view about the time when the question of a mail subsidy was being mooted.

Those that think that Crown Colony Government in Australasia is an anomaly ought to favour the taking over of any islands under Imperial administration . . .

We could not well raise the question officially but perhaps you might find an opportunity of stirring it up on your side.

If you think the time inopportune, it would be well always

to bear it in mind and take advantage of any moment when it may be proposed to your Ministers with better success.[10]

The immediate problem of Annie remained, but:

The new line of steam communication, which has just started, has assisted me in solving the difficulty.[11]

At a cost less than previously expected, the governor was able to send Judge Docker, a District Court judge, assisted by "three gentlemen, learned in the law", to the island. Economy dictated that the visitors would undertake the specific task of Annie Christian's trial, and more generally:

I have thought it well to begin by instructing them to enquire into the possibility of raising a revenue locally, and into the other matters referred to in my despatch number 6 on 2 December 1893. I hope their report will assist me in framing measures for improved administration, which I will submit for your Lordship's approval after visiting the Island.[12]

Annie was at last duly tried on 6 June 1894 on a charge of infanticide. The jury found her not guilty of that charge, but guilty of "Concealment of Birth". The sentence was nine months' imprisonment with hard labour. This punishment was, in the absence of a prison, rather less condign than may be supposed: Annie was "placed with a respectable family not belonging to the community". The family's home was appointed to be a "House of Correction" and the paterfamilias, John Cole, to be the keeper thereof.

The symptom having been dealt with, the commissioners moved on to examine the disease. Their report was sent to the Colonial Office in October 1894. They estimated about £200 a year could be raised in local revenues, but this would only go halfway to meeting the amount estimated to be needed for the "improved administration" which the commissioners recommended. They proposed an elected council, "presided over by a Chief Administrator" elected by the council, which would have the charge and maintenance of the roads and public buildings, and the administration of the public land, and which would collect the island's revenue. The governor should appoint a resident magistrate, with criminal jurisdiction over:

> ordinary crime, and with power to impose prison sentences of up to three years; capital cases and serious crimes would be dealt with either by special commissioner or by a Court in New South Wales.

> The magistrate should also have a civil Jurisdiction of up to £200, with a right of appeal to the Governor on questions of law. All laws in force were to be repealed and consolidated by the Governor who will reserve to himself the sole power to legislate for the dependency.

Additional revenues would be raised from specific customs duties on certain articles: "and perhaps an ad valorem duty on all other imports". Also from an assessment on stock, and a charge for timber cut on the public lands.[13]

Downing Street was unmoved by the Docker report.

> I do not understand that there exists in Norfolk Island any tendency . . . to commit acts of serious crime; such acts are I believe rare . . . no sufficient case has been made out to justify me in asking the Lords Commissioners of the Treasury to sanction the expenditure . . .

Within the Colonial Office, internal minutes in November 1894 re-emphasised the long-held view that Norfolk Island was a nuisance, and that New South Wales should be induced to take it off imperial hands.

> There can be little doubt that a more efficient administration of the law in Norfolk Island is absolutely required. The unsophisticated descendants of the mutineers of the *Bounty* do not pay their debts and at present there are no means to compel them . . . They are a curious community and despite their want of straightforwardness are law-abiding. It is remarkable that no provision is suggested for a policeman . . . but the Treasury may very likely think that the Island has no particular claim on the Imperial government which has already treated the Pitcairners liberally by moving them to Norfolk Island and giving them the convict buildings, stores etc. On the other hand it is rather disgraceful that there should be a British possession in which it is practically impossible to recover a debt. Nor was the Island annexed to please an Australian Colony – we might point this out in writing to Treasury . . . Wanted £200 a year for 5 years. We must go to the Treasury, though the chances of success are small. I only wish we could get this Imperial "preserve" annexed to one of

the colonies, but there are difficulties in the way which are almost insuperable – besides sentimentality.[14]

The forthcoming appointment of Viscount Hampden as governor provided a means by which the Colonial Office could advance its views, as Hampden had reached the same views even before he left England. He wrote to the Colonial Office from his English home in August 1895:

> to express an opinion that considerations of convenience, of local interests, of economical administration, and of the treatment of criminals, point to the desirability of persuading the Government of New South Wales to assume the charge of Norfolk Island; and it is upon this point specially that I desire your opinion before I leave for Sydney.[15]

The Office was, of course, avid in its concurrence.

> I am to observe, in the first instance, that Her Majesty's Government would regard with much satisfaction the taking over of the administration of Norfolk Island by the Government of New South Wales and Mr Chamberlain [the secretary of state] is glad to find that this view appears to be shared by yourself... Mr Chamberlain will be glad, therefore, if, on your arrival in New South Wales, you will take the whole matter into your consideration; and will favour him with your opinion, after consultation with your Ministers, as to the best course to be adopted.[16]

Almost immediately after his arrival in New South Wales, Hampden was able to telegraph London on 13 December 1895 that "Ministers agree in principle transfer of Norfolk Island" but, as previously, money was what lay between agreement in principle and agreement in fact.[17] The New South Wales Premier, George Reid, was explicit in his comment to Hampden on 31 December 1895 that "of course the transfer would be made so that the Island would become part of New South Wales and subject to its laws" because a transfer on that basis would bring to the Treasury "a fund in connection with the Pitcairn Islanders; this, I presume would be handed over to us for administration too".[18] And it was certainly Hampden's intention that the re-transfer to New South Wales would involve an annexation – a draft Order in Council prepared for Hampden in New South Wales and sent by him to the Colonial Office "to be issued when arrangements are complete for the transfer of the Island" included the following form of words.[19]

> Now, therefore, we do hereby order and direct that immediately upon and from and after the proclamation of this our Order in the Government Gazette of New South Wales, the Island called and known as Norfolk Island shall be transferred to, *and shall thereupon be annexed to*, the Colony of New South Wales . . .[20]

Not forgetting the most important point, Hampden's draft Order in Council concluded:

> And we do further order and direct that our Governor of New South Wales shall, immediately upon such proclamation as

aforesaid of this our Order, transfer to the Government of New South Wales the fund known as the Pitcairn Island Fund now vested in him or under his control, for the purposes of the income therefrom being applied towards the due support of the governing and social institutions that may be introduced into or made applicable to the said Island.[21]

Consistently with the intention that the colonial ministry would take control of the island, Hampden on 4 February 1896 appointed the New South Wales minister for lands, the Honourable J H Carruthers MLA, and Mr Charles Oliver, as commissioners to conduct a further general enquiry into the island's affairs. Oliver visited the island, but Carruthers did not. The commissioners reported promptly just over a month later. Carruthers's covering letter to Hampden of 9 March 1896 dealt with the financial implications of the proposed transfer to New South Wales.

> I gather, however, from my interviews with your Excellency, that the Imperial authorities are averse to any continued charge towards the local government of the Island; and in view of this fact, and also the probability that a revenue will be obtainable sooner or later from various local sources, I desire to suggest that the sum of £2,000 cash contribution be paid by the Imperial government, as its quota towards the expenditure to be incurred in governing the Island through this Colony . . . In case of any serious trouble on the Island (and possibly it might occur sooner or later) the people of New South Wales will be far from tolerant to any movement on the part of the New South Wales government to despatch

either military or police to the Island. It would be argued that it was not the business that the taxpayers of New South Wales paid their forces to do, and all eyes would be turned to the [imperial] fleet at our doors, to whose maintenance we contribute what to us is a large sum, £37,000.[22].

This line of argument pointed to a different conclusion from the premier's assumption of only two months earlier that the transfer of the island would "of course" involve annexation to New South Wales. Carruthers' point was that the imperial authorities should continue to bear ultimate financial responsibility for the island and, therefore, should continue to bear ultimate political responsibility as well. The Carruthers and Oliver report dated 10 March 1896 (though in fact presented to the governor the previous day, 9 March), diplomatically refrained from casting the argument in financial terms, as Carruthers's covering letter did, but the report did provide the political premise on which that financial conclusion was based.

> In regard to the contemplated permanent change, we respectfully point out that the application of the laws and system of governance in the colony of New South Wales would not prove suitable to the Island community, and, further, it is desirable to introduce a form of government which, while being effective, will not be altogether dissimilar to what the people of the Island have been accustomed to. This, it is thought, could be done by the Governor continuing his present independent control and authority, under advice from the New South Wales ministers. The local administration to be entrusted to a Government Resident.[23]

The political point had been pressed on the governor by his New South Wales ministers even before the delivery of the commissioners' report on 9 March 1896: on 5 March, Hampden's dispatch to the secretary of state sought to retract the earlier annexation proposal.

> My Ministers are advised by their law officers the draft Order in Council for the transfer of the administration of Norfolk Island to New South Wales transmitted to you under cover of my despatch of 20 January last, will in its present form subject the Island to all the laws of this Colony, and as they [the ministers] consider that many of the laws of New South Wales are not adapted to the community of Norfolk Island, they are of the opinion that proceedings for the transfer should be deferred until further consideration can be given to the form of the document effecting it.[24]

That deferral lasted longer than anticipated, as at this point New Zealand made a late bid for transfer of the island to that colony, the correspondence spanning the period March to July 1896, and ending on a familiar note: Chamberlain cabled to the New Zealand governor that "£2,000 required immediately [for] repair of buildings", and New Zealand's reply was that "Government have nothing more to say".[25]

After further exchanges between Hampden and Downing Street, the New South Wales proposal firmed up. Hampden telegraphed Chamberlain on 14 October 1896 that "Ministers propose that administration only should be transferred, legislative powers remaining as before... Complete annexation to New South Wales or future federal body to be postponed till Colonial Government think it desirable".[26]

This reflected the premier's advice to the governor on the previous day, 13 October, that:

> The question as to the future government of Norfolk Island has been seriously considered by Ministers, and I beg to acquaint your Excellency with the result of our deliberations.
>
> Whilst ready to assist your Excellency, in fact to be your Excellency's advisers on all matters of concern respecting the Island, we foresee great difficulties in the way of legislation either by the Governor with our advice or by the legislature of the Colony.
>
> We propose, therefore, that the Island should not be annexed formally to New South Wales, and that our services should be administrative only, legislation being conducted as formerly ...
>
> It should be understood, however, the Island is, as part of the arrangement, secured to New South Wales, or the future Federal body, when it is found expedient to ask for its annexation.[27]

The final step occurred on 15 January 1897, when a further Order in Council was made under the *Australian Waste Lands Act 1855*. The 1856 Order in Council was revoked, the separate office of Governor of Norfolk Island was abolished, and the Order provided that "the affairs of Norfolk Island shall henceforth, and until a further Order is made in that behalf by Her Majesty, be administered by the Governor and Commander-in-Chief for the time being of the Colony of New South Wales and its dependencies". The governor was empowered to make laws for the peace, order, and good government of Norfolk Island, and in the meantime existing laws were continued in force.

This was all precisely in accordance with the political accommodation reached between the imperial and New South Wales governments, even to the allusion in the Order of the premier's understanding that the island be "secured" to New South Wales, or to the future federal body "when it is found expedient to ask for its annexation".

> And whereas it is expedient that other provision should be made for the Government of Norfolk Island, and that, in prospect of the future annexation of that Island to the Colony of New South Wales, or to any Federal body of which that Colony may hereafter form part, *in the meantime* the affairs of the Island should be administered by the Governor of New South Wales as herein provided.[28]

In the light of the historical material referred to above, it is inarguably the case that the 1897 Order in Council not only did not annex Norfolk Island to New South Wales, but that it was unequivocally intended – after lengthy consideration and much correspondence – to avoid annexation.

The 1897 Order in Council remained in force until 24 July 1901. On that date a further Order in Council under the *Australian Waste Lands Act*, which was made on 18 October 1900, came into force. The only difference between the 1897

Order and the 1900 Order was terminological: the former referred to the Governor of *the colony* of New South Wales, whereas the latter referred to the Governor of *the state* of New South Wales, reflecting the differences in title arising from the fulfilment of Federation. Accordingly, the 1900 Order, like the 1897 Order, did not annex the island to any other polity. Consistently with that position, the re-definition of the boundaries of the states to be done in 1900 in preparation for Federation by Order in Council under the *Colonial Boundaries Act 1895* did not include Norfolk Island within the boundaries of New South Wales. New South Wales was defined as being:

> all that portion of Our territory of Australia or New Holland lying between the one hundred and twenty-ninth and one hundred and fifty-fourth degrees of east longitude, and northwards of the fortieth degree of south latitude, including all the islands adjacent in the Pacific Ocean *within the longitude and latitude aforesaid*, and also including Lord Howe Island, being in or about thirty-one degrees 30 minutes south, and the one hundred and fifty-ninth degree of east longitude, save and except those parts of Our said territory of Australia or New Holland which are called respectively "the State of South Australia", "the State of Victoria" and "the State of Queensland".[29]

Norfolk Island is situated in longitude 167° 57' E, and therefore Norfolk Island did not fall within the boundaries of New South Wales at Federation.

The final steps in the island's underlying constitutional history came in 1913 and 1914. In 1913 the Commonwealth

Parliament enacted the *Norfolk Island Act 1913*, which declared Norfolk Island "to be accepted by the Commonwealth as a Territory under the authority of the Commonwealth by the name of Norfolk Island". The Act was not to come into force until "the King has been pleased to place Norfolk Island under the authority of the Commonwealth".

As the recitals to the *Norfolk Island Act 1913* express, the terminology used in the Act reflected that of section 122 of the Constitution, which provides:

> The Parliament may make laws for the government of any territory surrendered by any State to and accepted by the Commonwealth, or of any *territory placed by the Queen under the authority of and accepted by* the Commonwealth, or otherwise acquired by the Commonwealth, and may allow the representation of such territory in either House of the Parliament to the extent and on the terms which it thinks fit.[30]

On 30 March 1914 the fourth and final Order in Council was made under the *Australian Waste Lands Act 1855*. The Order, after reciting the relevant provisions of the *Waste Lands Act*, the 1856 and 1900 Orders in Council (but not the 1897 Order), Commonwealth Constitution and the *Norfolk Island Act 1913*, provided that: "Norfolk Island is hereby placed under the authority of the Commonwealth of Australia". The antecedent Order in Council of 18 October 1900 was revoked. The new Order in Council was to come into force on the date fixed by the governor-general for commencement of the *Norfolk Island Act 1913*, which was 1 July 1914.

Norfolk Island therefore became, on 1 July 1914, a "territory" within the meaning of section 122 of the Constitution and has remained so ever since.

But did Norfolk Island thereby become a "part of" the Commonwealth?

During the parliamentary debate on the second reading of the Norfolk Island Bill 1913, the responsible minister thought not.

> In 1897, the question was raised as to what should be done with the Island, and it was pointed out that there could be no annexation by New South Wales or the Commonwealth except by an Act of the Imperial Parliament. But, by an Order in Council the Island can be placed under the control of the Commonwealth. When that Order in Council is issued, the administration of Norfolk Island will be transferred from the Governor of New South Wales to the Commonwealth, and become a Territory which will be administered by the Commonwealth in accordance with section 121 [sic] of the Constitution.[31]

These views echoed those of Sir Robert Garran (see below), which are in turn consistent with the opinions expressed by the imperial law officers at around the turn of the century. In 1896 the law officers (Webster and Finlay) advised the Colonial Office that imperial legislation, not an Order in Council, would be required to annex the island to New South Wales, but the proposal that the island should not be formally annexed to New South Wales; the services of the government in that colony to be administrative only "could be effected by Order in Council". That was of course what was done in 1897. In 1902 the law officers (Finlay and Carson) advised the Colonial Office that, in view of the enactment of the *Commonwealth of Australia Constitution Act*, Norfolk Island *could* be annexed to the Commonwealth without imperial legislation, because, unlike in the case of the Colony of New South Wales, there was no statutory restriction as to the extension of the boundaries of the Commonwealth by means of Order in Council under the *Colonial Boundaries Act 1895*.

As a matter of historical fact, however, no such boundary extension occurred. Instead, the course ultimately adopted was described in the 1902 opinion, but in view of the conclusion already reached in the opinion that the available mechanism arose under the *Colonial Boundaries Act 1895*, its legal effect was not expressly advised on.

> If annexation without an Imperial Act of Parliament was impossible, whether there were any, and if so, what objections to transferring the administration of Norfolk Island from the Government of New South Wales to the Government of the Commonwealth, by revoking the Order-in-Council of 15 January 1897 [under the *Waste Lands Act 1855*] and substituting for it an Order in Council placing the Island under the authority of the Commonwealth under the provisions of section 122 of the Constitution?[32]

The clear implication is that this course (which was the course followed) would not be effective to annex the island to the Commonwealth, whereas an Order in Council under the *Colonial Boundaries Act 1895* would have been.

It follows that "... the Commonwealth Parliament's relationship to [Norfolk Island] is not that of a Sovereign exercising power over part of its own territory but that of a Sovereign exercising power over territory committed to its government but not as part of its territory".[33]

The opinion of the imperial law officers was consistent with the views of Sir Robert Garran, in his capacity as secretary to the Federal Attorney-General's Department, expressed in 1905.[34]

> 7 October 1905. The Prime Minister. These papers are referred by the Prime Minister for advice as to the possible modes of annexation of Norfolk Island to the Commonwealth, and their consequences.
>
> Norfolk Island was originally part of the Colony of New South Wales.
>
> The Imperial Act 6 & 7 Vic c35 empowered the Queen by Letters Patent to sever Norfolk Island from New South Wales and annex it to Van Diemen's Land, and this was done, as from 29 September 1844, by Letters Patent dated 24 October 1843.
>
> The Australian Waste Lands Act 1855 (18 & 19 Vic c56), section 5, empowered the Queen by Order in Council to separate Norfolk Island from Van Diemen's Land, and "to make such provision for the government of Norfolk Island as may seem expedient".

Accordingly, by Order in Council dated 24 June 1856 (SRO Rev Vol 5 p.129) it was ordered that from the date of proclamation of the Order in New South Wales, Norfolk Island should be separated from Van Diemen's Land and be a separate settlement and provision was made for its government.

That Order in Council was repealed by an Order in Council (SRO 1897, p.504) dated 15 January 1897, made under the Australian Waste Lands Act 1855, which – after reciting that "it is expedient that other provision should be made for the government of Norfolk Island and that, in prospect of the future annexation of that Island to the colony of New South Wales or to any federal body of which that colony may hereafter form part, in the meantime the affairs of the island should be administered by the Governor of New South Wales as herein provided" – provides for the administration of the affairs of the Island accordingly.

Norfolk Island is therefore a separate settlement, for the government of which the King may provide by Order in Council under the Act of 1855, and which at present is administered by the Governor of New South Wales under the Order in Council of 1897.

The possible modes of annexing Norfolk Island to the Commonwealth appear to be:

(1) to make it a territory placed by the Queen under the control of and accepted by the Commonwealth

– or otherwise acquired by the Commonwealth (Constitution section 122);

(2) to place it within the limits of a State of the Commonwealth (Constitution section 123); and

(3) to admit it as a new State of the Commonwealth, subject to such terms and conditions as Parliament imposes (Constitution section 121).

The Island could apparently be made a territory under the control of the Commonwealth by the joint operation of an Imperial Order in Council and a Commonwealth Act. The effect of this would be that the Parliament could make laws for its government, and it would be a dependency of the Commonwealth, not a part of the Commonwealth itself, and the general laws of the Commonwealth would not be in force in the Island to any further extent than the Parliament thought fit to provide – nor would it necessarily be within the Commonwealth tariff fence. In other words, it would be in the same relation to the Commonwealth as British New Guinea will be if the Papua Bill (1) is passed.

The Island could be placed within the limits of a State by the procedure provided by section 123 of the Constitution – in conjunction with an Imperial Order in Council – and the effect would be that it would become part of the State and of the Commonwealth.

[Vol 5, p.89] RR Garran (2) Secretary, Attorney-General's Department.

(1) Enacted as the Papua Act 1905.

(2) This opinion was endorsed "I agree". Forward to the Honourable the Prime Minister, by Mr Isaacs, Attorney-General.

Chapter 2

Pitcairn Island

> It was now the depth of winter . . . we had hard gales and high seas . . . with frequent thunder and lightning, sleet, and rain . . . we discovered land to the northward of us. Upon approaching it the next day, it appeared like a great rock arising out of the sea . . .

Thus wrote Captain Philip Carteret as he described the discovery of Pitcairn Island in his "Account of a Voyage Around the World" published in an edition of *Hawkesworth's Voyages* in 1773. He named the island Pitcairn Island after Robert Pitcairn, the midshipman who first sighted it.[1]

Pitcairn Island is one in a group of four uninhabited islands known as the Pitcairn Group, comprising Pitcairn, Henderson, Ducie and Oeno Islands. Now inhabited, it is a small, volcanic island located in the South Pacific Ocean at latitude 25° 4' S and longitude 13° 6' W, considerably closer to the coast of Chile, South America, and the British Naval Base at Valparaíso than to Sydney, Australia. It is an irregular shape, about 3 kilometres long by 1.5 kilometres wide with an area estimated to be about 454 hectares. About 35 hectares of the land is flat or flattish, the remainder being rolling hills and steeply sloping land with sheer cliffs bordering the ocean, making access extremely difficult. There are a number of "walleys", eroded rock indentations that carry water when it rains, but only one spring of fresh water, known as Browns Water, which flows intermittently.[2]

On 28 April 1789 Fletcher Christian, master's mate, and a number of members of the crew of HMAV *Bounty* seized command of the ship from Captain William Bligh during a voyage to the South Pacific Ocean to collect breadfruit plants. Aware of their need for a place of refuge, the mutineers, led by Christian, sailed the South Seas in search of a suitable place to hide. One month later they landed on the island of Tubuai where they received a mixed welcome from the Polynesian inhabitants. For nearly four months the mutineers maintained a troubled existence on Tubuai, both vacating and returning to the island to live. Finally, the problems that beset them proved too difficult and on 17 September 1789 the *Bounty* sailed from Tubuai bound for Tahiti. The mutineers decided to split into two groups, so they divided the supplies, with each group taking its share. One group stayed in Tahiti and the second group of nine mutineers sailed on to find a safe haven where they could settle in peace.

When the British Government heard about the mutiny after Bligh's return, Captain Edward Edwards of HMS *Pandora* was sent to the Pacific to find and apprehend as many of the mutineers as possible. At Tahiti, Edwards found three of the mutineers, who surrendered to the law on 23 March 1791. After a further search, the *Pandora* left Tahiti with fourteen prisoners on board. The voyage home, however, ended in disaster as the ship was wrecked on a coral reef in the Torres Strait on 29 August 1791. Thirty of the ship's company were drowned and four of the prisoners. The survivors made their way in the ship's boat to Timor, arriving there sixteen days later. The ten surviving mutineers were subsequently returned to England where they were landed in chains on 19 June 1792. Six of the prisoners were found guilty of mutiny at the trial and sentenced to death by hanging and four were acquitted. Mercy was recommended for two of the guilty prisoners – Peter Heywood and James Morrison – and they escaped the gallows.[3]

The second group of mutineers who sailed with the *Bounty* were Fletcher Christian, Edward Young, John Mills, William Brown, John Williams, Alexander Smith (later known as John Adams), Matthew Quintal, William McCoy and Isaac Martin. Six Polynesian men, nineteen women, and a young baby, making a total of 35 persons, accompanied the mutineers when the *Bounty* left Tahiti on 23 September 1789. But six of the women were reluctant to leave their families, so they were put ashore on Mo'orea, a small island 14 kilometres from Tahiti. After a voyage of almost 5,000 kilometres in four months in search of sanctuary, the crew at last found the place that Carteret had described: Pitcairn Island. The 28 persons on board landed on the rocky shore of what was later called Bounty Bay on 23 January 1790, nine months after seizing HMAV *Bounty* from Captain Bligh.[4]

Following a safe landing of the people and all the useful contents of the ship, the *Bounty* was set on fire to avoid discovery and it sank in the bay. This event, however, did not preface a trouble-free life for the new settlers. Arguments between the men – often over women – frequently ended in murder. Others died as a result of accident, suicide, or poisoning from home-brewed alcohol, so that by 1800 John Adams was the only man left of the original group of settlers. With him were five or six women and twenty children. It then fell to Adams to guide the tiny community into the future. It is said that he experienced dreams of hellfire and damnation and that the day of judgement was nigh. These dreams prompted him to turn away from the anarchy of the past and to lead the people by example towards Christianity and a truly Christian life. Evidence of his success in this role was recorded in the observations made by visitors to Pitcairn in later years.[5]

Discovery, rules, and regulations

In 1808 Captain Mayhew Folger of the American sealer *Topaz* discovered John Adams, the lone survivor of the *Bounty* mutiny, and the progeny of the mutineers on Pitcairn Island. The following year Folger advised the British Government of his discovery, reporting that he had found the people to be "very humane and hospitable". No subsequent action was taken by the government to apprehend Adams as it had done nearly twenty years earlier when fourteen of the mutineers were found in Tahiti.

Again in 1814 Sir Thomas Staines, Captain of HMS *Briton* and Captain Pipon of HMS *Tagus* came upon Pitcairn Island by chance and were amazed to find it inhabited by English-speaking "natives". When the two captains went ashore, the Islanders were very concerned that the ships had come to arrest John Adams for his part in the mutiny. Although Adams said he was prepared to go back to England to stand trial, Staines and Pipon declined his offer. They had observed the "pious manner" and "correct sense of religion" of the Islanders' behaviour during their visit as well as the "exemplary conduct and fatherly care" with which Adams controlled the community. As Pipon later recalled, it would have been an act of great cruelty and inhumanity to have taken him from his family as the settlement would probably have been annihilated.[6]

Another 24 years were to pass before Britain recognised Pitcairn Island. When Captain Russell Elliott of HMS *Fly* visited the island in 1838, he issued a set of "hasty regulations" as a basis upon which the Islanders could order their community. This, however, was not an instruction from Britain but was a request by the Islanders themselves.

These events raised the question: Why did the government, after Folger's and Staines's reports, fail to take action to enforce British law as it had done twenty years earlier? And why was Britain reluctant to annex Pitcairn Island as a British colony? Various explanations may account for these outcomes.

A period of western colonial expansion began around the middle of the fifteenth century as most emerging nation-states sought to extend their power to settle and exploit recently discovered lands for resources that would benefit the home state. Voyages of colonisation and conquest were arranged by England and France, Portugal, Spain, and the Low Countries following Christopher Columbus's discoveries in 1492.

In the sixteenth century colonisation sped westward across the Atlantic Ocean to North and South America, and in the east, Portugal entered the Indian Ocean where it established three settlements on the west coast of India (now New Goa).

Portugal was without competition until Holland, then the leading trader and commercial power, chartered the Dutch East India Company in 1602. This company founded Batavia (now Jakarta) and the settlement became the centre of trade with China, Japan, India, and the Middle East.

Around the same time, the London East India Company, chartered in 1600, joined other foreign merchants to take advantage of opportunities for trade in the east as commercial activity significantly grew over the next two centuries. While European merchants trading throughout the Pacific were familiar with the islands, their home governments generally chose not to establish colonies. Although an increasing number of traders and missionaries were already in the area, the absence of political rivals and the lack of commercial interest in territorial expansion until around 1870 meant that nation-states did not begin to acquire colonies. Britain, then the dominant naval power in Oceania, was under pressure from the Australasian colonies, which sought the protection of the home government to prevent other nations from claiming the island first. One explanation for this apparently late colonisation of the Pacific may be that home governments considered the expense of setting up colonial administration would not be sufficiently profitable. Another reason was probably connected with the emerging political doctrine of liberalism, which rejected the system of mercantile regulation and prompted schemes for free trade in commerce. In early nineteenth century Britain there was an influential body of opinion that opposed the acquisition of new territory since these people considered the cost of its administration to Treasury would reduce the financial benefits of an open market for British enterprise. In 1838, therefore, when Elliott assumed the power of the British Crown to place its "stamp of authority" on Pitcairn Island, it was not as part of British foreign policy.[7]

The situation in Europe at the turn of the nineteenth century was for Britain a period of extreme conflict with France. The two enemies were engaged in war from 1793 to 1815, the years during which Folger, Staines, and Pipon made contact with the Pitcairn Islanders. This war was the most costly ever fought by Britain, and the burden on the economy caused a financial crisis. Fully committed at home, the Colonial Office as a result probably did not welcome Elliott's action on Pitcairn.[8]

In addition to this, nearly twenty years had passed between the trial and conviction of the *Bounty* mutineers, and the Staines and Pipon reports to London and memory of the event had faded from the public mind. This, together with the war with France, probably influenced Britain's decision to pass over the discovery, the inevitable expense and cost on resources for such an expedition seeming unjustified.

Exploration of the Pacific Ocean had, by the turn of the century, revealed the vast number of islands, the people, and the potential for trade. News of the new island community soon filtered back to Europe, where responses to the discoveries differed. Merchants and traders saw the Pacific as a profitable commercial opportunity, but others, such as the philosophers of the Enlightenment and religious organisations, saw the discoveries in different terms.

From the middle of the sixteenth century to the end of the eighteenth century, an intellectual revolution evolved which was concerned with two distinct but related movements: the Scientific Revolution and the social movement known as the Enlightenment. The scientific theories developed in 1543 by Nicolaus Copernicus, a Polish astronomer, and then a century later by Galileo and the scientist Isaac Newton, revealed the universe as an orderly system able to be analysed and understood by rational man. The second movement, a rationalist approach developed during the course of the Scientific Revolution, was applied to philosophy and society. As a result, men of the Enlightenment thought if the physical universe could be completely understood through the power of reason then the same method could be applied to the workings of society. Since man was as much a part of nature as the planets and nature was conceived as something orderly and good, it was only necessary to discover the "natural laws" which govern society and to use them as a standard against which all institutions could be measured. The doctrine of liberalism grew out of the ideas of the new learning, and the characteristic feature of its expression was a belief that it would lead to progress or perfectibility.[9]

Earlier reports of visits by explorers to islands in the Pacific Ocean and the initial welcome and generosity extended to them may have seemed to the men of the Enlightenment to exemplify the kind of ideal society living in a state of nature that they had been seeking.

In contrast to the ideas of the new learning that allowed man to make judgements about himself and society, religious organisations adhered to the authority of the church and to the teachings of the Bible.

The London Missionary Society, an interdenominational evangelical organisation formed in 1795, was the first of a number of religious organisations to send missionaries to

Oceania to extend the influence of the Christian gospels. The society sent 29 clergy with Captain James Wilson in command of the *Duff* in 1796. They established a mission on Tahiti, received with courtesy, and were told that they might take as much land for the mission as they pleased. Other acts of courtesy and generosity were reported by the missionaries. It transpired, however, that the Islanders had no intention of giving the land to the mission but allowed the visitors to stay in order to take advantage of the property, such as axes, knives, and cloth, the English could provide. On getting to know the Tahitians, the missionaries described their moral character as being "awfully dark". Aside from the "apparent mildness of their disposition and the cheerful vivacity of their conversation, no portion of the human race was ever, perhaps, sunk lower in brutal licentiousness and moral degradation than these isolated people".[10]

The clergy had witnessed what they considered to be the "moral depravity" of the native seen in their customs of theft, fornication, and infanticide.[11]

There were, as a result, conflicting views expressed by philosophers in Europe and by the Christian Church about the new societies in the Pacific, but each found support for their theories in their interpretation of the island life-style. It was against this background that the discoveries on Pitcairn Island were made, as well as future decisions about the island's society.

Glowing reports received in London of the Pitcairn community emphasised the piety and simplicity as well as the generosity and morality of the people. The small society appeared to be living in a state of innocence and harmony, attributes lauded both by philosophers and the church in England. The news probably confirmed each party's philosophical theory: this, indeed, was an ideal community living according to the principles of Christianity.[12]

The settled state of the island together with Britain's foreign policy and the current financial strain on its economy no doubt influenced the Colonial Office's design to refrain from annexing Pitcairn in the early nineteenth century.

Prior to 1838 seventy vessels from around the world landed on Pitcairn Island. Most of the visitors were commercial vessels searching for whales, seals, or opportunities for trade, and warships from London or the various British naval bases that were patrolling the sea for signs of foreign ships. Life on the island, therefore, was well known to the outside world as well as being reported in the Sydney press.[13]

Staines had recommended the community as being worthy of the attention of religious organisations in 1814, and the London Missionary Society sent books and Bibles by various ships to assist the people in their religious education. The Calcutta Committee of the Society for Promoting Christian Knowledge sent the merchant vessel *Hercules*, which sailed under British colours from Calcutta to Pitcairn in 1819, and Captain James Henderson's positive account of the visit was subsequently published in *The Calcutta Journal*.

During the next decade three men who were not related to the mutineers settled on the island: John Buffett and John Evans in 1823 and George Hunn Nobbs in 1828. Nobbs was to become an influential leader and cleric on Pitcairn and later on Norfolk Island. Buffett and Evans, two English seafarers, accompanied by Captain Hall of the British whaler *Cyrus*, landed on Pitcairn on 10 December 1823. The Islanders had requested the British Government to send them a teacher for several years, and they welcomed Buffett as their pastor and schoolmaster, and John Evans was also permitted to stay. Both men were allotted land, married, and began families.[14]

George Hunn Nobbs was born in Ireland but grew up in Yarmouth, England. He arrived on Pitcairn as an Englishman. Nobbs served in the British Navy for a number of years and later received a commission in the Chilean Navy. He was aware of the reputation of the community on Pitcairn and was attracted to it as a good place to settle. In the company of an American, Noah Bunker, on a voyage from Peru, the two men sailed to Pitcairn Island, where they arrived on 28 October 1828, in search of seals. The Islanders, however, were suspicious of the new arrivals and their motives in wishing to stay on the island, and considerable discord arose as Nobbs challenged Buffett's position as teacher and pastor. Nobbs, whose education was superior to that of Buffett, gradually took over his role and became influential in the community. Bunker had been ill for some time and died soon after landing.

Until the time of his death on 5 March 1829, John Adams remained the leader of the community, but soon after his death Nobbs was in control of island affairs. He caused a brief code of laws to be written that were intended to supersede Adam's personal and sometimes arbitrary decisions. They provided penalties for murder, theft, adultery, and removing a landmark. The punishment for murder was death and for theft, three-fold restitution. For adultery (which apparently meant fornication) there were two penalties: the first offence, for both parties, was marriage within three months; for the second, if the parties refused to marry, the penalties were forfeiture of lands and property and banishment from the island. The offenders were to be tried before a bench of three elders, who pronounced the sentence. The penalty for removing a landmark did not appear in external records. Although these rules did not have the official sanction of the British Government, they marked the first attempt to codify a set of rules for the Pitcairn Islanders.[15]

Indications that all was not well on Pitcairn had been received by Sir John Barrow, second secretary to the First Lord of the Admiralty. He urged the Colonial Office to take action to preserve the integrity of the Islanders and to assist them to transfer to another place. Captain AA Sandilands of HMS *Comet* was subsequently directed by the Governor of New South Wales to proceed to Pitcairn with orders to transport the people to Tahiti, the agreed location. On arrival at Pitcairn on February 1831, Sandilands found the Islanders reluctant to leave their home. Drought conditions on the island and the inevitable effect on resources convinced him to persuade the people to move. The transfer to Tahiti was, however, short. The Islanders were "discontented and unhappy" due to the immorality of the Tahitian life-style, and they contracted serious illnesses while they were there. The previous arrangement for possible return to Pitcairn was accepted six months later and the whole population arrived home on 2 September that year.[16]

The unfortunate experience on Tahiti thus foreshadowed their unwillingness to make the transfer to Norfolk Island.

The arrival of another visitor from Tahiti in 1832 was the imposter Joshua Hill, who claimed to be a representative of the British Government. During his five years on the island, Hill managed to deceive Captain Fremantle of HMS *Challenger* about his credentials and to dominate and frighten the people by laying down harsh rules written and imposed by himself. He also connived to banish the three Britons – Buffett, Evans, and Nobbs – to neighbouring islands for nearly a year. Although he controlled the community for some time, news of his offensive action was communicated to the British authorities, and he was deported in 1837. Joshua Hill never had the force of British law.[17]

Perhaps it is not surprising to find when Captain Elliott arrived in Pitcairn on 13 November the following year that he was greeted by an anxious and unhappy people. As well as the fearful experience with Hill, the Islanders had suffered unwelcome harassment from "lawless strangers" on whale ships who insulted them. They were taunted with jibes that they had "no laws, no country [and] no authority" that the sailors could respect, and they pleaded with Elliott to provide them with a structure for their regulation and government. Although he was aware of Britain's policy on annexation, Elliott, nevertheless, felt it his "duty" to provide some protection for the Islanders, and he acceded to their request.[18]

When the mutineers (who were British subjects) settled on Pitcairn in 1790, the island became a British possession and in the protection of the Crown.[19] Thus at the time of Elliott's arrival in 1838, the 99 inhabitants, who had already felt themselves to belong to Britain, were already British subjects. In consequence, Elliott drew up a legal framework that was pertinent to the needs of the community upon which the Islanders could govern themselves. He also presented a flag, the Union Flag, to the community as a symbol of British authority, and he presided over the first election of officers for which he had provided in the laws and regulations. This document addressed the main issues that were likely to arise on the island.

The regulations entitled "all inhabitants" – men and women – who had reached the age of eighteen years to vote, and they provided for the election of a chief magistrate, who was to hold the main authority on the island. He was to be assisted by a council of two "natives", one to be appointed by himself and the other to be the choice of the people. Other residents who had lived on the island for five years were also eligible to vote but could not hold office. This is apparently the first British settlement to include women in the franchise. The chief magistrate was to settle all disputes that arose with the advice of his council, but if any proved too difficult he was to refer the matter for a decision by the captain of the next naval vessel that arrived.

In essence, Elliott devised a structure of ten laws for the order and good government of the community, for the control of animals, and a system of education. He also included rules for the protection of trees and timber for building, the cultivation of land, and maintenance of landmarks. The final two laws dealt with trading with ships, intoxicating liquor, and a law to cover the use of public tools: the anvil and the sledgehammer.[20]

The first law instructed the magistrate to hold a public meeting if he received a complaint, and on hearing both sides of the argument, he was to submit it to a jury. He was to be treated with respect at all times in his administration of fines levied and all public works executed. He could not assume any power or authority without the consent of the majority of the people. In addition to these instructions, the magistrate was to keep a public journal in which the laws were to be recorded. These were to be read to the people regularly to inform them of the rules, so that they could not plead ignorance of the law if a crime was committed. This journal was also to be shown to visiting naval captains.

The next three laws were concerned with the control of animals: dogs, cats, and hogs. The owners of dogs were liable to pay fines or damages if they were found chasing goats, fowls, or hogs. For chasing a goat, the dog owner was required to pay one and a half dollars, one dollar to the owner and the half dollar to the informant. If a goat was injured or killed, the owner of the dog was required to pay damages, but if it was uncertain which dog had been the culprit, all dog owners had to contribute to the cost of damages. This law, however, had no effect if the goat was on uncultivated land. Persons who owned fowls or hogs that fossicked for food in the bush could take a dog with them to round up their animals, but if this dog damaged other animals then the owner was liable to pay for the damage.

Cats, on the other hand, were to receive preferential treatment. Fines for killing a cat seemed disproportionately severe to those for injury to goats, fowls, and hogs. If a child under ten years was responsible for killing a cat, the child received corporal punishment, but if the offender was between ten- and fifteen-years-old, the fine was 25 dollars, half of the fine to be given to the informant and half to public funds. Other offenders and all masters of families convicted of killing a cat were to pay a fine of 50 dollars, again half to the informant and half to the public. It seemed greater value was placed on cats than on dogs. On the other hand, cats probably ate the rats that escaped from the numerous visiting ships and, therefore, played an important role in the community.

The law for hogs provided compensation for owners whose property had been damaged by another pig. The property owner could claim the pig for himself if he witnessed the damage and if he was reliably informed that the pig was responsible for the damage. It was an offence to neglect to report damage done by a pig to property and to the property owner. If the person who failed to report the offence was found guilty of neglect, then he must pay the damages sustained by the property owner.

Instructions for the children's education were detailed in he fifth law. A school was to be kept to which parents were obliged to send their children. Students aged from six to sixteen years were to attend school from seven o'clock to midday on weekdays. They were required to learn the alphabet before starting school, but no curriculum was stated. The head teacher, George Hunn Nobbs, was paid a salary, and he was to be assisted by other suitable persons named by the chief magistrate. He was also required to monitor the children's progress and maintain the correct teaching standards. Parents paid one shilling per month for each child's tuition, or the equivalent in local produce.

Miscellaneous issues in the sixth law included rules about land cultivation and collecting timber for buildings and windbreaks, cases before the magistrate, church wardens, and restrictions about shooting. Clearing of land for cultivation was permitted after the public was notified, and any person could cut and collect the wood if desired. But if any person took more than was needed to build a house, then the remainder was to be given to the next person who wished to build a house. This rule applied to miro (Podocarpus ferrugineus) and borob timber only. With regard to windbreaks, any homeowner could nominate particular trees to be left standing in order to act as a windbreak for the house or plantation. These trees were not to be cut down, even though they may be growing on another's land. The protected tree of miro or borob pine is a native forest tree of New Zealand important to Māori. It is tall but slow growing, and the wood is strong and hard and is now popular for weatherboards and floors. Borob timber has not been identified under that name in any encyclopedias or other works. The Māori may have named both timbers, and visitors to Pitcairn may have taken seeds or seedlings with them as gifts to the inhabitants.[21]

At public meetings no person could mention an old dispute in order to incriminate another with a view to affecting a case before the magistrate. Anyone so doing was to be given an appropriate fine awarded by the jury.

The magistrate was to appoint four churchwardens on the first day of each month, and finally, any person found shooting or in any way killing white birds "(unless it be for the sick)", was to pay a fine of one dollar for each bird killed.

The seventh law was concerned with the use of wood. Logs cut for fencing were not to be suitable for building houses. The magistrate was to appoint four men to inspect the logs and any found to be serviceable for building dwelling-houses were to be confiscated and given to the next person ready to build a house. A time limit was placed on building a home, and if the wood was not used in the specified time, it was to be given to the next home-builder. There were a number of restrictions on the age, use, and potential of timber cut, with the view to protecting the growth of young trees for future house-building.

Rules for landmarks were set out in the eight law. All landmarks were to be inspected on the first day of January each year by the new magistrate or the men deputed by him to carry out the inspections. The magistrate was to ensure lost landmarks were to be replaced at the first opportunity.

Laws for trading with ships and the use of public tools were governed by numbers nine and ten. The purchase and sale of spirits from visiting ships was prohibited. It was unlawful to obtain spirits from vessels visiting the island and any person found guilty of committing this offence was to be "severely punished" by a jury. Women were not allowed to board a foreign vessel without the permission of the magistrate. If permitted, they were to be accompanied by the magistrate or four men appointed by him to look after the females. The tenth law required anyone taking the public anvil or sledge-hammer for his own use to return it to the blacksmith's shop as soon as possible. If the tools were lost, the last user was to replace them and pay a fine of four shillings.[22]

The ten laws as drafted by Elliott were not written in professional legal language. The wording and content of the laws suggests that they may have been discussed and requested at a public meeting of the Islanders then compiled by Elliott, either at the meeting or later on. Although there was unanimous praise for the honesty, integrity, and harmony in the community by visitors to the island, the fact that penalties for wrongdoers were thought necessary and were provided by the law suggests that international reports and perceptions of this society may have been slightly exaggerated. Perhaps the early reputation of the community meant that philosophers and humanitarians saw what they wanted to see on Pitcairn Island. But, in reality, the Islanders were subject to the same human frailties as people in other societies.

Walter Brodie, an English traveller and writer, spent sixteen days in Pitcairn in 1850. During the visit Brodie recorded the laws of the Islanders drafted by Captain Elliott "word for word", and they were later published in his work *Pitcairn's Island and the Islanders* in 1850. In addition to the above laws, Brodie noted rules of another "code" that were not included in the laws but which were, nevertheless, in use upon the island. The code, as recounted by Brodie, was long and detailed, and it contained rules that applied to public works and the church, the school, and other miscellaneous matters.

Part of the code on public works stated who would undertake public work, as well as the terms on which land was to be transferred. One member of each family was obliged to carry out public work, and land was to be equally divided between the children and the family. When a man married, he took his share of his father's land and his wife took her proportion of her father's land. In this way the young couple had immediate access to property and thus were able to begin a new generation. If a property bordered the seashore, Brodie noted it might seem "strange" but even the rocks on the seashore were shared as private property as they were valued for the collection of sea-salt.[23]

Divine service was held in the schoolhouse that was large enough to accommodate 200 people. Two services and a Sunday school were performed on Sundays. The communion services, gospels, epistles, and litany were read during the month and the Islanders were questioned on the catechism at the afternoon service held on the first Sunday of the month. Brodie also wrote that Eucharist could not be administered as George Nobbs was not an ordained minister. Funerals were attended by all persons on the island. Girls could not marry under the age of sixteen years.

Details of hours and attendance, fees, curriculum, and holidays were outlined in the section dealing with the school. This section was considerably expanded to recount many other aspects of life on Pitcairn. Information about agriculture, animals, fish, and other produce was recorded, as well as details about houses, clothing, and the general health of the inhabitants. "Strangers" were welcomed and given lodging in a private home out of generosity but also to keep a close watch on them. Produce that was available for trade was listed in the miscellaneous section. Brodie wrote a comprehensive account of these "good people", who impressed him as being "unlike any that [he] had seen or heard of before". His work was published in 1851 and further captured the attention of English readers keen to learn more about the small community on Pitcairn.[24]

The foundation of the Pitcairn community and the subsequent development of its Constitution, both on that island and later on Norfolk Island, are unlike other settlements of the British Empire.[25]

Prelude to transfer

After Elliott's departure in 1838, a number of British naval ships called at Pitcairn. Captain J Shepherd of HMS *Sparrowhawk* landed on 9 November 1839 and during the next three days heard "several cases" that were "submitted to him for decision". He also addressed the community on "various subjects connected with their welfare" and "distributed rewards among the children of the school according to their respective merits". The ship departed that evening.

Over the next decade seven British naval ships visited Pitcairn. HMS *Curacoa* under Captain Jenkin Jones arrived from Callao on 18 August 1841 and found the community in the grip of an epidemic of influenza. The ship's surgeon, Dr Gunn, tended twenty cases of the virus and prescribed drugs from the medicine chest intended as a gift to the Islanders as well as medicine from the ship's supply. Captain Jones met the people that were well enough to attend at the schoolhouse and addressed them upon "several subjects connected with their welfare". He read a letter from Admiral Ross and presented "a variety of very useful articles" that were gifts from the Admiral and others for distribution among those present at the schoolhouse. No details of the content of Ross's address were noted in the Pitcairn Island Register, but the health of the sick had improved and heartfelt thanks were extended to the surgeon. The ship sailed on 20 August with the community's prayers for the preservation of the "worthy captain, officers and crew". The Register, begun in 1790, is the earliest known record of the inhabitants and events on Pitcairn Island.[26]

On 5 March 1843 Captain Thompson of HMS *Talbot* landed on the island. He presided over some of the most pressing cases before departing for Valparaíso, apparently on the same day.

The following year Captain Henry Hunt of HMS *Basilisk* arrived at the island on 28 July, bringing with him gifts from the British Government. He stayed four days before sailing to the Sandwich Islands. During the visit Hunt disposed of such cases as were presented to him for "adjudication" and the ship surgeon vaccinated 60 Islanders and prescribed medicine for several cases of sickness. On 31 July 1844 Hunt assembled the inhabitants and made some alterations to the rules, and suggestions about others, "for the improvement of the community generally", but the changes were not recorded in the Register. Lastly, he appointed a "commercial agent", but again, no reason for this appointment was given in the Register.

Three years were to pass before Captain Woodbridge of HMS *Spy* was reported offshore on 26 February 1847. The ship was greeted with a "grateful explanation" from the people, who were in great need of a surgeon to attend an injured young man. As he was "pressed for time", Woodbridge announced that the ship would depart that afternoon for Valparaíso. Before leaving, however, he concerned himself with the welfare of the inhabitants and took notes of their needs.

Captain H J Worth of HMS *Calypso* called at Pitcairn on 9 March 1848. The captain and a party of officers landed, taking with them "two large whaleboats and several large cases of useful articles" as gifts for the Islanders from various residents in Valparaíso. Although the captain and crew were urged to remain, the ship sailed two days later.

The last two ships recorded in Brodie's account of the Island Register arrived in 1849. The cannon of HMS *Pandora* was heard on the island early in the morning of 10 July. Captain T Wood disembarked with John Buffett, who had gone to the Sandwich

Islands about six months before. Wood brought letters from the Consul-General at Tahiti and several other persons who offered to provide land for any of the Pitcairn families who wished to emigrate there. He informed the community of the concern for their welfare and that he would stay onshore until the next afternoon to give them time to deliberate on the contents of the proposal, but it was refused. With the community's prayers for their safety, the ship departed as arranged.

A month later Captain Fanshawe of HMS *Daphne* from Valparaíso landed on Pitcairn on 11 August. The captain took ashore gifts of livestock, several boxes of "acceptable articles", and a large case of books from the Society for Promoting Christian Knowledge that were gratefully received by the people. Although pressed to stay, the ship sailed for Tahiti the next day.[27]

The records in the Register indicate that all captains and crew were solicitous for the welfare of the community and anxious to report their needs and conditions on the island to those at home. Only seven naval vessels landed on Pitcairn from 1839 to 1850, thus there were many months when there was no contact with Britain, but the people survived without official assistance. During the intervals between visits, however, the Register's entries suggest that the naval captains were diligent in carrying out Elliott's instructions of 1838 to provide assistance and protection for the community. In addition, the visits by the naval ships and gifts sent to the Islanders by the British Government indicate Britain's support for Elliott's 1838 actions. Aside from contact with the British Navy, 239 commercial vessels called at the island during the same period, and most of them obtained supplies from the island's limited resources. This, together with the hardships caused by almost constant sickness, drought, storm, shortage of food, and an infestation of worms that destroyed the potato crop, made this period an extremely difficult one for the inhabitants. The health of the people deteriorated, and thus the land was not properly maintained.[28]

As Brodie later reported, the Pitcairners had realised the import of their situation by the time of his arrival in 1850. The natural increase in the population, the area of the tiny island, and the shortage of food and water meant that emigration would "become a matter of necessity". On his return to England in 1851, Brodie publicised the state of conditions on Pitcairn and enlisted the help of various philanthropists and initiated the Pitcairn Island Fund to raise funds for the community. A great deal was now known overseas about the island's affairs, and transfer to Norfolk Island seemed to be a possibility.[29]

Reports about the community being "cramped for room" continued, as did offers of land on other islands, but the Islanders desired a place where there were "no inhabitants to interfere with them". In his work of 1851, Brodie had suggested the possibility of Norfolk Island as a suitable place for the Pitcairners to settle if the British Government decided to close the penal colony there.[30]

The visit in August 1852 by the commander-in-chief of Her Majesty's Naval Forces in the southern Pacific, Vice Admiral Sir Fairfax Moresby, marked another step in the progress towards the relocation of the Islanders. His report to London again confirmed the opinions of earlier visitors as to the island, stating that it was "impossible to do justice to the spirit of order and decency that animates the whole community". Observing the health of the people and the gravity of the need for supplies of food and water, Moresby was convinced that the community must either emigrate or perish. The community's desire for an ordained pastor was also made known to him, thus George Hunn Nobbs sailed with him to London later that month. Nobbs was well received in London, where he addressed the first meeting of the Pitcairn Island Fund Committee and met with officials in the Colonial Office. On 30 November 1852 Nobbs was ordained "Chaplain of Pitcairn's Island" by the Bishop of London with a salary of £50 per annum paid by the Society for Promoting Christian Knowledge. After an audience with Queen Victoria and the Prince Consort and the completion of his ordination, he returned to Pitcairn with Admiral Moresby on 15 May 1853.[31]

Before Moresby's departure, he suggested that a public meeting be convened to consider his advice on "several important points" connected with the "peculiar state and position" of the Islanders. A letter from the magistrate (Arthur Quintal, *Jun*) and two councillors, Thomas Buffett and Edward Quintal, dated 18 May 1853 informed Moresby that his "wise proposition for the amendment of certain laws relative to the duties of the Chief Magistrate" and the age to which councillors were eligible to hold office had been "unanimously agreed at a public meeting and that the proposed changes would be implemented at the first opportunity". The letter also requested aid from the British Government to transfer them to Norfolk Island or some other "appropriate" place.[32]

This request was made earlier to B Toup Nicolas, the British Consul at Raiatea in the Society Islands when he arrived in HMS *Virago* in January 1853.[33]

The chief magistrate, Matthew McCoy, conveyed the people's willingness to leave Pitcairn but on condition that the British Government would cede Norfolk Island to them. On 5 July 1854 Nicolas forwarded the reply from the Colonial Office to the Islanders. The letter stated that Norfolk Island could not be "ceded" to the Pitcairners, but that grants of land would be made to the new settlers and that it was not intended that others would be permitted to settle at present. The Islanders, however, understood that "indefeasible right and title" to Norfolk Island had already been given to them.

When Captain J S Fremantle of HMS *Juno* conveyed the contents of Sir William Denison's "summary of arrangements" to be made at Norfolk Island for occupation of the Pitcairners during his visit in September 1855, the Islanders were, in view of their past experience on Tahiti, at first uncertain about leaving Pitcairn. On hearing the summary, however, the people "seemed greatly reanimated by the assuring prospects" of life at Norfolk Island and the Islanders subsequently agreed to the transfer.[34]

C H Currey, an Australian historian and teacher, argued in 1958 that misconceptions may have arisen from Denison's original directive that indicated that land on Norfolk Island would be exclusively possessed by the Pitcairners. He pointed out that "cession implies much more in law than possession however lawful", and that the Islanders might well have "failed to appreciate the distinction". Currey also quoted from one of Denison's letters that so "judicious an officer" as Captain Fremantle would not have made any "unauthorised cession".[35]

Perhaps Denison's understanding of the terms to be offered to the Islanders was that they should have exclusive occupation rather than exclusive possession or cession. Regardless of the possible confusion over possession or cession in 1855, the matter had already been settled by the British Government through Nicolas's letter of 5 July 1854.

A dispatch from the Right Honourable Henry Labouchere, secretary of state for the colonies, to Denison dated 21 January 1856 informed him that following the removal of the convicts from Norfolk Island it was intended that the Pitcairners be transferred to that island. It was further stated that it would be "desirable" that Norfolk Island be placed under Denison as Governor of New South Wales but not annexed to New South Wales. This was to be achieved by an Order of Her Majesty in Council under the powers granted by the *Australian Waste Lands Act 1855*, 18 and 19 Vic c.56 s.5 dated 24 June 1856. This order separated Norfolk Island from the colony of Van Diemen's Land and created Norfolk Island, a "distinct and separate settlement" under Governor Sir William Denison.[36]

Labouchere concurred with Denison's suggestion that it would be necessary to supply sufficient provisions for the settlers until they had time to grow their own food and that the land should not be sold to "any other races" until the "present experiment be fully tried". Other arrangements regarding the distribution of land to families, the authority to settle disputes, and other unforeseen problems that might rise would be left for Governor Denison. In conclusion, Labouchere remarked that although it was probably "unnecessary", he recommended the Islanders "whose past history and conduct have so greatly excited the sympathy of the people of this country to [Denison's] especial care and protection". The reference in the dispatches from both Denison and Labouchere to the "experiment" of the transfer of the Pitcairn community to Norfolk Island and the government's concern to isolate the society from any outside influence that might corrupt the "innocence" and "integrity" of the settlers suggests that their focus was more than just a satisfactory resettlement of the Islanders. The language used in testimonials written by official and other visitors about the community implied a knowledge of the ideas that grew out of the Enlightenment. In 1838 Captain Elliott found the Pitcairners "an interesting community" that had preserved their "deservedly high character for exemplary morality, innocence and integrity". Ten years later Captain Worth wrote that "they are the most interesting, contented, moral and happy people that can be conceived" and Admiral Moresby in 1852 wrote in a similar vein that "it would be impossible to do justice to the spirit and order of decency that animates the whole community".[37]

Many other examples of such praise for the Pitcairners can be found in the records. The consistently positive opinions of various observers, indeed, suggested that many in the outside world saw the island community as the ideal society that conformed to their notion of natural principles of Christian theology.

Following the decision to transfer the Pitcairners to Norfolk Island, the necessary arrangements were made and the entire community of 193 persons embarked on the *Morayshire* on 3 May 1856. After a "perilous journey" of around 5,000 kilometres the Islanders landed on Norfolk Island on Sunday 8 June 1856 in a state of extreme fatigue.[38]

Although the journey of nearly five weeks had been a trying one for the passengers, most of whom suffered from severe seasickness, a child was born to Miriam Christian. The child, a boy, was christened Reuben Denison after the Governor of New South Wales. Despite general exhaustion, the new settlers held a special service of thanksgiving to which Captain H M Denham of HMS *Herald* was invited. Denham, who had been appointed to survey the island prior to the arrival of the new settlers, was present to welcome them. After attending the service, he described it as being an "exemplary manifestation of habitual piety". By the end of June 1856, Denham and others stationed on the island departed, and the 40 men, 47 women and 107 children commenced a new life and the beginning of the third settlement on Norfolk Island.[39]

Chapter 3

Norfolk Island

Norfolk Island was discovered by Captain James Cook on 10 October 1774. The island was uninhabited. Cook claimed it as a British possession.[1]

So far as is known, the island was not revisited by Europeans and remained uninhabited until 6 March 1788. On that date, a small party of convicts and others landed on the island. This occurred pursuant to the instructions given to Captain Arthur Phillip to "send a small establishment" to Norfolk Island.

From 1788 until 1844 Norfolk Island was either part of or attached to New South Wales. For example:

- 1786 – Phillip's first commission of 12 October 1786 appointed him governor of "our territory called New South Wales . . . including all the islands adjacent in the Pacific Ocean within the latitude aforesaid of 10o 37' S and 43o 39' S . . . ".[2] Norfolk Island lies in latitude 29o 4' S.
- 1787 – in constituting the criminal jurisdiction of New South Wales, Norfolk Island was described as "one of

the . . . islands adjacent to the eastern coast of New South Wales".[3]
- 1795 – the statute 35 Geo 3 c.18, relating to criminal courts on the island, referred to Norfolk Island as being within the authority of the governor or lieutenant governor "of the Eastern Coast of New South Wales, and the Islands adjacent thereto".[4]
- 1831 – Governor Bourke's commission as Governor of New South Wales dated 25 June 1831 referred to Norfolk Island as being included in the territory of that colony. Other governors' commissions did not.[5]
- 1843 – under powers conferred by the statute 6 and 7 Vic c.35, Queen Victoria appointed by commission that from 29 September 1844, Norfolk Island "shall cease to belong to the colony of New South Wales, and shall be taken to be a part of the colony of Van Diemen's Land".[6] This step was taken for reasons connected with the organisation of the penal settlement.

Norfolk Island was occupied, principally as a penal settlement but with some free settlers, from 1788 until 1814, and again from 1825 until early 1856. It was unoccupied from 1814 until 1825, but was visited from time to time during this period by British warships.

Not later than 6 March 1788, Norfolk Island was validly established as a "settled" British colony, and that proposition is non-justiciable. As was said by the High Court in 1992:

Under British Law in 1788, it lay within the prerogative power of the Crown to extend its sovereignty and jurisdiction to territory over which it had not previously claimed or exercised sovereignty or jurisdiction. The assertion by the Crown of an exercise of that prerogative to establish a new Colony by "settlement" was an act of State whose primary operation lay not in the municipal arena but in international politics or law. The validity of such an act of State (including any expropriation of property or extinguishment of rights which it effected) could not be challenged in British Courts . . . The result is that, in a case such as the present where no question of constitutional power is involved, it must be accepted in this Court that the whole of the territory designated in Phillip's commissions was, by 7 February 1788 (the date on which Phillip read his Second Commission dated 2 April 1787, "with all due solemnity", at Sydney Cove), validly established as a "settled" British Colony. [7]

The legal status of Norfolk Island remained unaltered until after the enactment on 16 July 1855 of the *Australian Waste Lands Act 1855* (Imp) (18 and 19 Vic c.56). The main thrust of that Act was to empower colonial legislatures to "repeal, alter or amend" previous imperial Orders in Council regulating "the sale and other disposal of the waste lands of the Crown". An important exception to that general principle was to reserve to the Crown the future disposition of Norfolk Island:

> provided always, that it shall be lawful for Her Majesty at any time by Order in Council to separate Norfolk Island from the Colony of Van Diemen's Land, and to make such provision for the Government of Norfolk Island as may seem expedient. (First Proviso to Section 5.)

This was followed by the making of an imperial Order in Council on 24 June 1856, by which Queen Victoria separated Norfolk Island from the colony of Van Diemen's Land and from the jurisdiction of the governor of that colony and ordered that the island:

> shall be a distinct and separate settlement, the affairs of which shall, until further order is made in that behalf by Her Majesty, be administered by a Governor, to be for that purpose appointed by Her Majesty . . .

It was further ordered that:

> (a) . . . the Governor and Commander-in-Chief for the time being in and over the colony of New South Wales shall be constituted and appointed, and he is hereby constituted and appointed, Governor of the said island called Norfolk Island . . .
>
> (b) . . . the said Governor . . . shall have full power and authority to make laws for the order, peace and good government of the said island, subject, nevertheless, to such rules and regulations as Her Majesty at any time, by any instruction or instructions, with the advice of Her Privy Council, under Her sign manual and signet, may think fit to prescribe in that behalf.

The policy motive for the making of the 1856 Order in Council is evident from the royal instructions issued under the Order in Council. Materially, these include the following provisions in respect of the power to make laws reposed in the governor by the Order in Council:

(a) In framing such laws as aforesaid you are to observe, as nearly as the circumstances will admit, the rules laid down by our Instructions under our Sign Manual and Signet addressed to you from time to time as Governor of New South Wales: And whereas the inhabitants of the said island are chiefly emigrants from Pitcairn's Island in the Pacific Ocean, who have been established in Norfolk Island under our authority, and who have been accustomed in the territory from which they have removed to govern themselves by laws and usages adapted to their own state of society, you are, as far as practicable, and as far as may be consistent with the regulation next preceding, to preserve such laws and usages, and to adapt the authority vested in you by the said recited Order in Council to their preservation and maintenance.

(b) And whereas you are further authorised by the said recited Order in Council to make grants of Waste Lands in the said Island . . . Now we do hereby further enjoin you to exercise the authority so vested in you, as far as you may find it practicable, in conformity with such laws and usages as aforesaid which you may find established among the inhabitants in question, as far as the same may be applicable to the subject.[8]

The historical fact underlying the Order in Council and the royal instructions was therefore the arrival in Norfolk Island on 8 June 1856 of the entire population of Pitcairn Island, who had embarked by arrangement with imperial authorities on the *Morayshire* on 3 May 1856. As mentioned in chapter 2, the population thus embarked numbered 193 persons, and a child (christened Reuben Denison after the Governor of New South Wales) was born to Miriam Christian during the passage.

The move from Pitcairn to Norfolk Island had been under active consideration, in Pitcairn and elsewhere, since at least 1853. At that date, Pitcairn's laws were still essentially the "hasty regulations" drafted on 29 November 1838 by Captain Russell Elliot of HM Sloop *Fly* at the request of the Islanders themselves and promulgated the next day. These were reproduced "word for word" by an English visitor, Walter Brodie, in his *Pitcairn's Island and the Islanders* (Whittaker & Co, London, 1851).

The only material change to the 1838 Constitution and Code of Laws prior to departure for Norfolk Island was the adoption in 1853 of recommendations made the previous year by Vice Admiral Sir Fairfax Moresby during a visit to Pitcairn in August 1852. These related to the duties of the chief magistrate, and the age at which councillors became eligible to hold office. A letter from the chief magistrate, Arthur Quintal, *Jun*, and two councillors to Moresby dated 18 May 1853 informed him that "his wise proposition for the amendment" of those laws had been "unanimously" agreed at a public meeting, and that the proposed changes would be implemented at the first opportunity.

The materials set out above accordingly constitute "the laws and usages" referred to in the 1856 royal instructions.

The adaptation of those laws to the Norfolk Island situation was remarkably slight, as a comparison will demonstrate. This was deliberate: Governor Denison travelled to Norfolk Island in September 1857 and on his arrival was provided with a copy "of the Laws and Regulations of the Island, being the same as those in force at Pitcairn". After a short voyage to New Zealand, Denison returned to the island in early October.

> My business . . . was not to devise some perfect scheme of government for this small community or large family, but to give them every help in the shape of advice. I was not, therefore, disposed to press changes upon them which I might think advisable . . .
>
> . . . I went with Mr Nobbs and the magistrate carefully over the laws which I intended to propose to the public meeting of inhabitants. I had drawn these out on my way from New Zealand, taking care to make the code as simple and as short as possible. I based it upon the rules which had been found to suit the habits of the people at Pitcairn Island, repealing, of course, those which had a purely local application, and inserting a few which bore upon the duties they would have to perform in their novel position at Norfolk Island. I made a few modifications in my draft at the suggestion of Mr Nobbs and the magistrate, and I inserted a law against the introduction of wine and spirits, analogous to the Maine Liquor Law . . . I left untouched the rule which gave the women, as well as

the men, a vote in the annual election of the Chief Magistrate. I hope, however, that this experiment on a small scale, will not be assumed as a precedent in favour of the claims now made on the part of our "better halves", to have their say in the government of the country, for I doubt very much whether, even among the primitive people of Norfolk Island, it would be found to answer if pushed at all beyond its present limit. I should most certainly not have proposed even this small amount of petticoat government, had I not found it already in existence.[9]

On 14 October 1857, at "a meeting of the heads of families", Denison:

pointed out to them that the Queen had given me power to make laws and regulations for them, but that I had also been directed to pay attention to their views and wishes; that in the preparation of the laws which I was about to read to them, I had been guided by those under which they had hitherto been living; that I had done away with a few which were only applicable to the state of things at Pitcairn Island, and that I had added one or two suited to the situation in which they were then placed. I read the laws over to them one by one, commenting upon each as I went along, showing how it was either an old law differently worded, or that it was, to a certain extent, modified. I explained more particularly each of the new laws, so that I felt sure that they not only comprehended the meaning, but the motive for its introduction . . . Having gone into these explanations, I asked them whether they had any observations to make, and whether they were willing to abide by the laws they had heard read; and I found that the general feeling was in favour of their adoption. They were then decided to be the laws of the land for the present . . . [10]

The laws so decided upon were commonly known thereafter as the 39 Laws. They were published in a supplement to the New South Wales *Government Gazette* on 30 October 1857.

The letters patent of 1843 referred to above, by which Norfolk Island was attached to Van Diemen's Land, expressly used the language of annexation:

Our said Island, called Norfolk Island, shall be severed from the Government of New South Wales, and annexed to the Government and Colony of Van Diemen's Land.

However, the Order in Council of 1856 equally expressly eschewed the language of annexation:

It is therefore ordered by Her Majesty, by and with the advice of the Privy Council, that from and after the date of the proclamation of this Order in New South Wales, the said Island called Norfolk Island shall be and the same is hereby separated from the said Colony of Van Diemen's Land (now called Tasmania), and that from the date aforesaid all power, authority and jurisdiction of the Governor, Legislature, Courts of Justice, and Magistrates of Tasmania, over the said island shall cease and determine. And it is hereby further ordered and declared, that from the date aforesaid the said island called Norfolk Island shall be a distinct and separate settlement, the affairs of which shall, until further order is made in that behalf by Her Majesty, be administered by a Governor, to be for that purpose appointed by Her Majesty, with the advice and consent of Her Privy Council.

Non-annexation in 1856 was a deliberate policy decision, as the correspondence set out below demonstrates.

On 25 December 1854, Sir William Denison, who then held the position of Lieutenant Governor of Van Diemen's Land but whose appointment as Governor of New South Wales had been foreshadowed, submitted in a dispatch to the Colonial Office:

> that Norfolk Island, as it comes within the geographical boundaries of the colony of New South Wales, should, when it ceases to be a convict establishment, be placed again under my jurisdiction, as I shall take an interest in the establishment of the Pitcairn Islanders, and shall have better opportunities of watching over them than can fall to the lot of the Governor of Van Diemen's Land. [11]

The Colonial Office's ultimate response to that proposal was dated 21 January 1856 and concluded:

> that after the removal of the last of the convicts, it will be desirable that Norfolk Island should be placed under your government as Governor of New South Wales [Denison having in the meantime taken up his appointment to the latter position], but not annexed to the latter colony as part of it; and I shall take the first opportunity of forwarding to you an Order of Her Majesty in Council for effecting that object, under the

powers created by the Act 18 and 19 Vict, c.56, s.5 [i.e., the *Australian Waste Lands Act*].[12]

In the meantime, however, Denison had changed his mind so that his views corresponded to the passage just quoted. In his dispatch dated 27 February 1856 (which was of course written before the above dispatch of 21 January 1856 reached him) he said:

> In a former Despatch from Van Diemen's Land, in December 1854, I suggested that the island should be retransferred to New South Wales. I wish now to modify this recommendation, and to suggest that Norfolk Island should not form part of any of the adjacent colonies, but should be kept altogether distinct from and independent of them. The effect of making it a part of any of these colonies would be to confer upon the legislatures the right of dealing with the people and the land according to their will and pleasure, and thus an opportunity would be afforded for interfering with the experiment which is now about to be made. Such interference could not be useful, and would, probably, be injurious. I would, therefore, press most earnestly upon your notice the propriety of withdrawing the island from the jurisdiction of adjoining colonies.
>
> The Governor General of the Australian colonies [i.e., Denison himself] might have a nominal jurisdiction, in order that the people should have somebody to whom they might make their wants known, and through whom they may correspond with Her Majesty's Government upon the subject of the changes in

the form of government which will in course of time become necessary, or upon such matters as they may not be able to arrange themselves.[13]

It was, therefore, consistent with the views both of the imperial authorities and of Denison that the 1856 Order in Council would refrain from annexing Norfolk Island to any other colonial possession.

The 1856 Order in Council was expressed to take effect upon its proclamation in New South Wales, which occurred on 1 November 1856.

From that time until the closing years of the century, the Norfolk people largely regulated their own affairs under the 39 Laws.

These laws vested the executive government of the island "during the absence of the Governor" (that is, for practical purposes, all of the time) in:

> a Chief Magistrate and two Assistants or Councillors, to be elected annually by the community as hereinafter directed.

Denison conceived of the arrangements made in 1856 and 1857 as experimental. He could say:

> nothing very definite as to the success of the experiment with the Pitcairn Islanders. I have had letters from various persons, each complaining of some particular grievance, but I have heard also that some of the inhabitants have succumbed to the temptations to which they have been subjected under their altered condition, but this was no more than might have

been expected. No possible training can eradicate from man the hereditary taint of his race; but I believe, or I may rather say, I know, that the community on Norfolk Island exhibits less evidence of this than any other with which I have ever been thrown in connection, and I hope that crimes of any magnitude are as yet unknown in this little dot of an island in the midst of the Pacific.[14]

Metropolitan concern about the state of the island, commencing in 1884, ultimately led to a constitutional change in 1897. As will be seen, however, this change – like that of 1856 – fell short of annexation of the island to another colony. The island remained a distinct and separate settlement.

The course of events was as follows.

In 1884, the then Governor Lord Loftus, visited the island. He was "very dissatisfied with the social and industrial condition of the inhabitants", and commissioned the visiting magistrate at Lord Howe Island, Henry Wilkinson, to inquire into and report upon the general state of affairs on the island. Wilkinson first reported in January 1885, and subsequently resided on the island for several months later in that year, which enabled him to prepare a second, lengthier report. The tone of Wilkinson's two reports may fairly be described as heavily critical.

Nevertheless, Wilkinson tried in his dealings with the Islanders to allay concerns stemming from the natural consequences of his recommendations. On a return visit, he addressed a public meeting held on 5 October 1886:

The subject that in the main occupied the meeting was the proposal by the authorities in England to hand over to New

South Wales, the general supervision of Norfolk Island affairs, but the point which, up to the time that the Assembly met, appears to cause the greatest anxiety, was as to what extent would such a change be likely to affect the constitution of the Island, as it at present stands. This point however was set at rest by Mr Wilkinson, who, as His Excellency the Governor's representative, had been send [sic] here to lay the matter before the people. From his statement it appeared, that no radical changes would be made in any way, without the consent of the inhabitants, that so far as was at present contemplated, the only change would be that His Excellency the Governor of Norfolk Island would in future be advised by the Government of New South Wales, instead of by the Colonial Secretary at home . . .[15]

Mr Wilkinson was also reported as "warmly advocating what he called a New South Wales protectorate", but this elicited some scepticism on the part of the principal of the Melanesian Mission, Dr Codrington, who stated that:

As regards the transfer of the Island Government now under consideration, he was strongly opposed to annexation in any form, and he was not quite certain what was meant by a protectorate . . . but if the alteration contemplated was simply only the substituting of the New South Wales for the Imperial Government . . . then it would make little or no difference to the existing state of things, and the community, by adopting this course, would probably be very much the gainer by the change, taking care however to preserve the present constitution".

Codrington "was repeatedly cheered while speaking", and consistently with the thrust of his remarks the meeting adopted the following resolution:

> The Community of Norfolk Island approve of the substitution of the Governor of New South Wales in place of the Imperial Government, provided always that no other change be made in the present constitution, without the sanction of the said community.

The mooted change did not take place at that time, but later events saw it revived.

In 1893 a case of alleged infanticide occurred, and the offender was tried on the island before a jury. However, the governor's request to the attorney-general of New South Wales, Edmund Barton, for advice led to an unexpected and unwelcome conclusion. Barton advised that the culprit had not been "tried and convicted by due legal process", and that in order for that to occur a properly constituted court would need to be sent to the island. That would require funds, and funds were not to be forthcoming from the imperial authorities.

The personal and the political converged over the infanticide case. As noted in chapter 1, the governor's financial embarrassment in dealing with it, and the wider question of the future of the island, were both addressed by sending Judge Docker, assisted by "three gentlemen, learned in the law" to the island on the "new line of steam communication, which has just started, [and which] has assisted me in solving the difficulty."[16]

Annie Christian was ultimately duly tried on 6 June 1894

on a charge of infanticide. The jury found her not guilty of that charge, but guilty of "concealment of birth".

In 1896 the imperial law officers (Webster and Finlay), were consulted by the Colonial Office about the terms of what became the 1897 Order in Council. Their report dated 10 December 1896, referred to the Colonial Offices' advice that:

> the government of New South Wales . . . now proposed that the Island should not be formally annexed to New South Wales; the services of the Government in that Colony to be administrative only, legislation to be conducted as formerly . . . it being however part of the arrangement that the Island was secured to New South Wales or the future Federal body when it should be found expedient to ask for its annexation.
>
> That it might be assumed that the object of this decision was to preclude the claim of New Zealand to have the Island annexed to that colony, and as Her Majesty's Government were anxious to believe the further responsibility respecting the administration of the Island, might be the best plan, if admissible, to vest the administration in the Governor of New South Wales in that capacity, and not as specifically Governor of Norfolk Island.
>
> That he [the Colonial Office official] was also to state that in view of the important business to be brought before Parliament next session, it was desired to dispense with any legislative measures that were not absolutely necessary, and that you would be glad if we could suggest any means by

which it might be possible to deal with this matter otherwise than by Imperial legislation.[17]

The law officers concluded that the desired end could be achieved by Order in Council (which was what occurred), but that annexation would require an imperial Act:

> Having regard to the very special terms of 18 and 19 Vict c.54, s.46 we feel a difficulty in advising that annexation can be properly effected without Imperial legislation . . . the point can be further considered when the necessity arises.

The necessity arose in 1902, when the imperial law officers (Finlay and Carson) were asked to advise on "proposals . . . as to the future administration of Norfolk Island" by the Governor of New South Wales and the Acting Governor-General of the Commonwealth of Australia. Their report dated 13 November 1902 noted that:

> the question as to the legal means by which Norfolk Island could be annexed to the Colony of New South Wales was submitted to our predecessors in office in 1896 . . .

> That from the form of those Reports it would appear that the obstacles in the way of annexing Norfolk Island to New South Wales by Order in Council under the Colonial Boundaries Act, 1895, were (1) the provisions of section 5 of 18 and 19 Vict, c.56 (the Waste Lands Act), and (2) the provisions of section 46 of the Bill scheduled to 18 and 19 Vict. c.54 which placed the boundaries of New South Wales upon a statutory basis

so as to prevent their being altered by Order in Council even with the consent of the Colony.

That he [the Colonial Office official] was to point out that in the case of the present proposal to annex Norfolk Island to the Commonwealth of Australia the second of the abovementioned obstacles would appear to have been removed by the enactment of the Commonwealth of Australia Constitution Act, 1900, and that it would further appear from the Report of our predecessors in office of the 10 December 1896, that the provisions of section 46 of the Bill scheduled to 18 and 19 Vict, c.54 was the chief of the two obstacles referred to.

That if this was the case it would, unless 18 and 19 Vict. c.56, section 5 was per se a fatal objection to the course proposed, appear possible, in view of section 8 of the Commonwealth of Australia Constitution Act, 1900, and section 122 of the Constitution scheduled thereto, to annex Norfolk Island to the Commonwealth by Order in Council *under the Colonial Boundaries Act, 1895* [emphasis added].[18]

Against that background, the law officers were asked to advise on four specific questions, namely:

(1) Whether Norfolk Island could be annexed to the Commonwealth of Australia without an Imperial Act of Parliament?

(2) If so, whether the annexation should be effected by

Order in Council under the Colonial Boundaries Act, 1895, or how otherwise?

(3) Whether such an Order in Council should make provision under 18 and 19 Vict, c.56, sections 4 and 5, for the interim Government of Norfolk Island pending legislation on that subject by the Commonwealth?

(4) If annexation without an Imperial Act of Parliament was impossible, whether there were any and, if so, what objections to transferring the administration of Norfolk Island from the Government of New South Wales to the Government of the Commonwealth by revoking the Order in Council of the 15th January 1897, and substituting for it an Order in Council placing the Island under the authority of the Commonwealth, under the provisions of section 122 of the Constitution?

The law officers answered these questions as follows:

(1) That in our opinion Norfolk Island can [original emphasis] *be annexed to the Commonwealth of Australia by Order* in Council without an Imperial Act of Parliament. There is no statutory restriction as to the extension of the boundaries of the Commonwealth of Australia and, having regard to the fact that Norfolk Island was acquired for the British Crown by occupation and not by settlement, it appears to us that the Crown has power by Order in Council to annex it to any other part of the Crown's dominions.

When Norfolk Island was first occupied, it appears to us that it was entirely at the disposal of the Crown, and the result of the Order in Council made under section 5 of the 18 and 19 Vict, c.56, was that it reverted to this position. We do not think that section 5 of the 18 and 19 Vict, c.56 prevents the Island, under these circumstances, from being at the disposal of the Crown – even if the power expressly conferred by that section is limited to making provision for the Government of Norfolk Island as a separate dependency. The annexation may be made in the manner proposed in virtue of the Crown's authority over territory acquired as Norfolk Island was, there being no statutory impediment to the extension of the boundaries of the Commonwealth.

(2) Subject to the consent of the Commonwealth of Australia the *annexation should be effected under the Colonial Boundaries Act 1895* [emphasis added].

(3) Such an Order in Council may make provision for the interim Government of Norfolk Island pending legislation on that subject by the Commonwealth. The Commonwealth Parliament might, however, pass an Act to take effect on the annexation, and this might perhaps be the more convenient course.

(4) The question does not arise.

The law officers' report of 13 November 1902 advised that the annexation of Norfolk Island to the Commonwealth of Australia should be effected under the *Colonial Boundaries Act 1895*, and that the consent of the Commonwealth to this course was needed. The latter requirement arose under covering clause 8 of the Constitution, which provides that:

> After the passing of this Act the Colonial Boundaries Act, 1895, shall not apply to any colony which becomes a State of the Commonwealth, *but the Commonwealth shall be taken to be a self-governing colony for the purposes of that Act* [emphasis added].

The emphasised words would have had the effect, in terms of the provisions of the *Colonial Boundaries Act*, of requiring the Commonwealth's consent to any alteration of the boundaries of the Commonwealth so as to encompass Norfolk Island.

As a matter of historical fact, such consent was not then, nor at any time afterwards, forthcoming. Nor did the imperial authorities seek to proceed in the manner proposed by the law officers.

What actually occurred was foreshadowed by Sir Robert Garran, in his capacity as secretary to the Federal Attorney-General's Department, in his advice to the prime minister dated 7 October 1905, set out in chapter 1.

> The Island could apparently be made a territory under the control of the Commonwealth by the joint operation of an Imperial Order in Council and a Commonwealth Act. The effect of this would be that the Parliament could make laws for its government, and that it would be a dependency of the Commonwealth, not a part of the Commonwealth itself,

and the general laws of the Commonwealth would not be in force in the Island to any further extent than the Parliament thought fit to provide – nor would it necessarily be within the Commonwealth tariff fence. In other words, it would be in the same relation to the Commonwealth as British New Guinea will be if the Papua Bill [enacted as the Papua Act 1905] is passed.[19]

Accordingly, when Norfolk Island became a "territory" within the meaning of section 122 of the Constitution on 1 July 1914, by Commonwealth Act and imperial Order in Council, the common understanding of the imperial law officers, Sir Robert Garran, and the federal minister was that the method adopted would not be effective to annex the island to the Commonwealth but instead would render the island subject to the "control" or "administration" of the Commonwealth.

Another way of expressing that common understanding is to say that on 1 July 1914 the island became a dependency of the Commonwealth, not a part of the Commonwealth.

The extent and nature of the Commonwealth's "control" or "administration" of the island after 1 July 1914 is outlined in what follows.

The long title of the *Norfolk Island Act 1913* is:

> An Act to provide for the acceptance of Norfolk Island as a Territory under the authority of the Commonwealth, and for the Government thereof.

The Act commences with a preamble which recites some of the principal features of the island's antecedent constitutional history, including the purport of the imperial statute 6 and 7 Vic c.35; the Order in Council of 24 October 1843 severing Norfolk Island from "the Government of New South Wales" and annexing it instead to "the Government and Colony of Van Diemen's Land", the provisions of the *Australian Waste Lands Act 1855*; the Order in Council under that Act dated 24 June 1856 separating Norfolk Island from Van Diemen's Land and erecting it as a "distinct and separate Settlement"; and the subsequent Orders in Council dated 15 January 1897 and 18 October 1900. The final two recitals are as follows:

> And whereas the Parliament of the Commonwealth is willing that Norfolk Island should be placed under the authority of, and accepted as a Territory by, the Commonwealth:
>
> And whereas by the Constitution it is provided that the Parliament may make laws for the Government of any Territory placed by the King under the authority of and accepted by the Commonwealth.

The Act was expressed not to come into operation "until the King has been pleased to place Norfolk Island under the authority of the Commonwealth, and the Governor General has been pleased, by proclamation, to fix a day for the commencement of this Act" (section 2). The first condition was satisfied by an Order in Council dated 30 March 1914, once more expressed to be made under the *Australian Waste Lands Act 1855*, by which His Majesty "hereby ordered, as follows: . . . Norfolk Island is hereby placed under the authority of the Commonwealth of Australia".

The second condition was satisfied by the governor-general's proclamation, which took effect on 1 July 1914.[20]

By section 3 of the Act:

> Norfolk Island is by this Act declared to be accepted by the Commonwealth as a Territory under the authority of the Commonwealth by the name of Norfolk Island.

Section 4 of the Act continued in force existing laws, subject to their alteration or repeal by ordinance made under the Act. Section 5 provided that:

> The Acts of the Parliament (except this Act) shall not be in force in Norfolk Island unless expressed to extend thereto.

The sidenote to this provision is "cf. 1905, No. 9, s.6", which is, consistently with Sir Robert Garran's comparison of Norfolk Island to the position of Papua, a reference to a materially identical provision of the *Papua Act 1905*.

The period between the establishment of the Commonwealth on 1 January 1901 and the coming into force of the *Norfolk Island Act 1913* on 1 July 1914 saw a good deal of interaction between state, Commonwealth and imperial authorities over the future of the island. The Governor of New South Wales, Sir Harry Rawson, on 7 August 1902 addressed a memorandum to the imperial authorities on the subject, a copy of which was provided to the governor-general. Sir Harry said in a minute to the governor-general:

> I am proposing to the Secretary of State for the Colonies that

Norfolk Island should be annexed to the Commonwealth, and be administered by the Federal Government. The present divided authority can never answer. The Postal arrangements, Customs and Tariffs, and presumably the Defence being worked by one, the administration by the other. I have ordered a Commission at once to go there and report on many outstanding questions. Would your Excellency inform me whether the Federal Government would be willing to take over the Island should the Secretary of State agree?[21].

These communications precipitated extensive correspondence, including obtaining the advice of the imperial law officers of 13 November 1902. There was, however, a delay on the part of the Commonwealth, because it awaited the result of the investigation by the Oliver Commission, referred to in Sir Harry Rawson's minute above. That commission reported in 1904, and after the death of the commissioner, a supplementary report was prepared in 1905 by the deputy administrator of Norfolk Island, Mr Houston, and John Watkins, parliamentary draftsman.[22] Oliver had reported that one of the means of achieving "a large output of the commodities of the Island" would be to attach the island to the Commonwealth. The 1905 supplementary report commented as follows:

> The question of cession to, or incorporation with, the Commonwealth is clearly one in which political considerations predominate.
>
> The Commissioner (Oliver) has, however, expressed certain views as to the effect of such incorporation on the output

of commodities which seem to call for remark, and has informed the Islanders that "chief amongst the benefits (of incorporation) was the relief from those Commonwealth duties of Customs which are now simply prohibitive".

As pointed out in a letter of Sir Edmund Barton to your Excellency, dated 30 July 1903, it is not a necessary consequence that, on annexation to the Commonwealth, the Norfolk Islanders would be at once free from the Commonwealth tariff . . .

A strategic consideration of imperial significance arose at this point, namely the Pacific Cable, which was laid inter alia from Fiji to Norfolk Island and from Norfolk Island to New Zealand, these stages being completed in 1902. This "All Red Line" was laid by a partnership or joint venture between the imperial, Canadian, Australian and New Zealand governments. A repeating station was located on the island. On 28 July 1906, the Governor of New South Wales in a dispatch to the secretary of state said:

> The transfer of the Island to the Commonwealth is, I consider, not only necessary but imperative for its defence as an Island, close to Australia, on which the telegraph cable is landed. Whether as a Crown Colony or properly annexed is for the Colonial Office to decide . . . [23]

The Governor General has forwarded me a letter – copy of which I enclose – informing me that, as far as possible, the Prime Minister promises that no alteration will be made in the laws governing Norfolk Island unless absolutely necessary . . . [23]

The immediate reason for this dispatch was to forward to the secretary of state a petition from a number of island residents stating their desire "to still remain a Crown Colony".

The letter from the governor-general to the Governor of New South Wales, referred to above, was dated 11 July 1906 and set out the advice received by the governor-general from the prime minister:

(1) I have the honour to inform Your Excellency that I am advised by my Prime Minister that the matter has received very careful consideration.

(2) While it is impossible even for Parliament to bind its successors, it is, as Your Excellency is aware, equally impossible for a Prime Minister to bind even his successor by any assurance in the form indicated in Your Excellency's despatch now under reply; but, so far as this is possible, effect can be given in another way to Your Excellency's wish that, as existing laws are satisfactory, they shall not now be disturbed, nor any change made hereafter, until the necessity for alteration is clearly shown.

(3) When, in terms of section 122 of the Constitution, Norfolk Island is placed by His Majesty the King under the authority of the Commonwealth, a Bill will be introduced accepting the territory; and, relying

upon Your Excellency's opinion that the present laws controlling the internal affairs of the Island are sufficient, my Ministers are prepared to agree that this measure will provide for the continuation of all existing laws without any other alterations than those of a purely formal character, which may be necessary for technical reasons consequent on the transfer of control.

(4) Of course, Parliament remains perfectly free to deal with its own Act whenever it thinks fit, but Your Excellency may fairly assume that no subsequent law altering the present conditions will be proposed unless there are strong reasons for change.

Having received this assurance, the governor telegraphed to the secretary of state:

I have received despatch from the Governor General stating that when Norfolk Island is placed by King under the Commonwealth under the terms of 122nd section of the Constitution a Bill will be introduced accepting the territory. As this session of Federal Legislature will end shortly and the elections will make uncertain the return of the present government, it is important that an Act should be passed at once and telegraphed to Governor General to enable present Federal Government to pass their Act of annexation before dissolution. Prime Minister agrees to Norfolk Island being governed by its present laws. It is necessary for its defence to be under the Commonwealth, as telegraph cable is now being landed on Island.[24]

This telegram therefore contemplated "annexation" by complementary legislation of the imperial and federal parliaments, rather than by way of an imperial Order in Council and federal Act.

No bill was introduced into Federal Parliament during the remainder of the parliamentary session, but after the elections a Norfolk Island Bill was introduced into the Third Parliament on 20 July 1909. The Second Reading speech of the minister for external affairs, Mr Groom, commenced by stating that:

> This most beautiful and fertile Island is exceedingly important to us because it is one of the stations of the Pacific Cable.

The Bill was not proceeded with, and lapsed when the Third Parliament was prorogued. The reason appears to be that New South Wales cast doubt on the propriety of the Bill. The Premier of New South Wales wrote to the prime minister in the following terms.

> Further, I am of opinion that section 122 of the Constitution, which provides for the Commonwealth making laws for government of a territory, was not intended to apply to a case where legislative and administrative control is being satisfactorily carried out by part of the constitutional machinery of a State, and the Executive authority of that State, moreover, has not asked to be relieved of its responsibilities.[25]

The federal attorney-general was asked to advise on this letter, and his advice dated 19 August 1909 stated that:

> The only sense in which it can be said that the legislative and

administrative control of Norfolk Island is being "carried out by part of the constitutional machinery of a State" is that, by Orders in Council of a provisional nature, the Governor of New South Wales for the time being is the Administrator of Norfolk Island.

Under the Australian Waste Lands Act 1855, the King has power to make such provision for the Government of Norfolk Island as may seem expedient.

In my opinion, the King has power to place Norfolk Island under the authority of the Commonwealth, and the Commonwealth Parliament, by virtue of section 122 of the Constitution, has power to accept it as a territory.[26]

Despite that opinion, this exchange led to further consideration by the imperial authorities of the precise manner of the proposed transfer. An opportunity to settle the matter arose in 1911, when the prime minister, Mr Fisher, was to visit London for the Imperial Conference of that year. A letter from Lord Chelmsford to the Colonial Office of 25 January 1911 prepared the ground.

> I had an interview with Fisher over the affairs of Norfolk Island and asked him to let me know exactly where things stood. I told him nothing could be more unsatisfactory than the present uncertainty . . . I . . . urged him to take over the Island. The difficulty in the way seems to be the giving of Free Trade to Norfolk Island. If the Island is to be Commonwealth Territory, he argues that it must be treated on the same lines

as Papua... Would it be well to consider an alternative policy of annexation to New Zealand? Probably New Zealand would jump at having the Island on our terms. I am writing to you, as I have as yet nothing definite to put into a despatch, and I want you to be aware of the position. [27]

A lengthy Colonial Office minute of March 1911 reviewed the situation in preparation for Mr Fisher's visit to London.

> Power to provide for the administration of the Island is given to His Majesty in Council by section 5 of the Imperial Act 18 and 19 Vict. Cap. 56. Under the authority given by this Act, Norfolk Island was administered up to 1896 by the Governor of New South Wales as Governor of Norfolk Island. In that year it was proposed to annex Norfolk Island to New South Wales so that the Government would rest with the Governor of New South Wales as such, that is to say, the Government would be conducted by the New South Wales Ministry.
>
> The Law Officers of the Crown, however, advised that the intention of the Act mentioned was that the territory should be governed under the Queen as a separate colony, and the original proposal was therefore modified, an Order in Council being issued on January 15 1897 under which the Governor of New South Wales was no longer made Governor of Norfolk Island but the government of Norfolk Island was vested in him as Governor of New South Wales.
>
> New South Wales has failed to do anything towards developing the Island and therefore, if any change is to be made, it would

seem to be in the direction of placing the Island under the administration of the Government of the Commonwealth.

In view of the Opinion of the Law Officers, to which reference has been made, it will be necessary that an Imperial Act should be passed for this purpose empowering His Majesty to place the territory under the authority of the Commonwealth. Sir Edmond [sic] Barton when Prime Minister of the Commonwealth, in 1903, and Mr Fisher in 1911, appear to have held that if Norfolk Island became a territory under their Government it must be treated like Papua to which it has not been found possible to concede a special tariff . . .

It might, therefore, if Mr Fisher cannot see his way to concede free trade, be suggested that the Island might be transferred to the government of New Zealand, which was formerly a claimant to it. They would no doubt gladly accept the Island and accord it favourable fiscal treatment. Sir Joseph Ward could be approached on the subject during his presence in England.[28]

Minuted in handwriting on this memorandum, by Sir C Lucas of the Colonial Office, is the comment: "On no account should we hint at its being annexed to New Zealand", and in the same hand, against the reference to Sir Joseph Ward (prime minister of New Zealand) is minuted "No".

On 1 March 1911, Mr A B Keith of the Colonial Office gave further consideration to Lord Chelmsford's views.

The remarks of Lord Chelmsford are interesting and I

completely agree with him in the view that free trade is essential if the state of the Island is to be improved. I do not think that it is fair or desirable to treat Norfolk Island like Papua. The circumstances of the two places are very dissimilar and therefore one cannot act as a precedent for the other. But I think it right, to avoid future difficulty, to point out that I am by no means certain that it will be possible to annex Norfolk Island to the Commonwealth. It is true that by Section 122 of the Commonwealth of Australia Constitution Act the Parliament may make laws for the government of any territory placed by the Queen under the authority of, and accepted by, the Commonwealth, and it has actually acted on that power in the case of the territory of Papua which has been placed under the Commonwealth. It has hitherto been assumed that it would be the case of Norfolk Island and that we could, on the passing of a Commonwealth Act, transfer the administration to the Commonwealth in the same way as the administration was transferred in toto when the Papua Act 1905 became law. But Papua was a British Colony pure and simple subject to the full control of the Crown unfettered by Act of Parliament in any form. In the case of Norfolk Island the action of the Crown is limited by the provisions of the Act 18 and 19 Vict. cap. 56 s.5 and cap. 54 s46, and you will see from the Law Officers' Opinions of October 31 and December 10 1896, which I annex, that in the opinion of the then Law Officers it was the intention of the imperial statute that Norfolk Island should remain a Crown Colony governed under the direction of the Queen in Council, and they were of the opinion then that even when the consent of the Colony of New South Wales, Norfolk Island could not be annexed to

New South Wales ... As a matter of fact it would be quite easy to pass a short Imperial Act if the question becomes pressing and I do not believe there is any likelihood at present of the Commonwealth legislating, but it seems to me essentially a question to be discussed with Mr Fisher when he is over here for the Imperial Conference. New Zealand is out of the question. [29]

A handwritten minute subjoined to this memorandum, initialled by Sir C Lucas, adds:

I think it is clear that if we are to get Norfolk Island annexed to the Commonwealth we must pass an Imperial Act. The matter should be discussed with Mr Fisher and we should press for "free trade".

In June 1911, Mr Harcourt of the Colonial Office discussed the matter in London with Mr Fisher.

Mr Harcourt has seen Mr Fisher and Mr Batchelor about Norfolk Island. They seem disposed to take the Island on the Secretary of State's condition of free trade with Australia, but will wait till they get back before deciding.

The Bill subsequently introduced into the Fifth Parliament of the Commonwealth in 1913 provided for free trade, to the extent that: "the produce of Norfolk Island coming direct to Australia to be admitted free in all cases in which there is not an excise duty on similar commodities here".

To that extent, the objective of the imperial authorities was achieved. However, nothing was said or done to contradict the imperial authorities' view that Norfolk Island could not be annexed to the Commonwealth absent an imperial Act (or, at the least, an alteration of the Commonwealth's boundaries by Order in Council under the *Colonial Boundaries Act 1895*). To the contrary, in the Second Reading Debate on the *Norfolk Island Bill 1913*, the minister for external affairs expressly referred to the fact that "there could be no annexation by New South Wales or the Commonwealth except by an Act of the Imperial Parliament".[30]

Chapter 4

Hope and Disappointment 1914 to 1939

The years between the transfer of the government of Norfolk Island to the Commonwealth of Australia in 1914 and the commencement of World War II in 1939 were categorised by a number of periods of economic optimism followed by periods of downturn and disappointment. While it was generally anticipated that the new relationship with Australia would lead to improvements in the island's economy through trade and the standard of the internal administration, this optimism was too often blighted by external events. The vagaries of the market in Sydney and elsewhere and the embargo on export of fruits and vegetables to New Zealand, as well as the incidence of disease and crop failure, drought, and world depression, all combined to hamper financial growth. Instability was the mark of this phase and the island's development. By 1913, on the other hand, the economy, despite its rickety progress, had improved to indicate a long-term upward trend in real income and living standards.[1]

World War I and its effect on the island, the withdrawal of the Melanesian Mission in 1920, and the appointment of Colonel E T Leane to the post of administrator and chief magistrate in

1924 were effects that had far-reaching consequences for the island population and the Constitution. A royal commission on Norfolk Island affairs in 1926 culminated in dismissal of Colonel Leane from his position and led to significant constitutional changes for the people in the 1930s. These changes occurred at the same time as the residents, in general, were experiencing the economic pain of the Great Depression. It was a time of extreme hardship, when fear about the future caused considerable tension within the community and a strained relationship with the authorities.

The *Norfolk Island Act 1913* was proclaimed and became operative from 1 July 1914, one month before Britain declared war on Germany on 5 August 1914. The new Act transferred the authority of Norfolk Island to the Commonwealth of Australia and it gave additional roles to the administrator who was also to be the chief magistrate. This move was significantly assisted by the continuation of Michael V Murphy's connection with the Islanders as the first administrator to act in the dual role. He was first known on the island as a government surveyor in 1903, before he was promoted to the position of deputy administrator in 1913 after William Houston's resignation. Following observations made by Atlee Hunt during his visit to Norfolk Island early the next year, Hunt recommended Murphy as the person who was "in every way suited" for the position as he carried out his duties with "ability" and "marked tact"; the next year the governor-general confirmed his appointment.[2] After the changeover the community generally accepted Murphy in the new role, as the people had known him for a number of years and he understood the community's special culture. This, no doubt, facilitated the period of transition for the island during the first years under the Commonwealth. But these years, on the other hand, were significantly affected by events in Europe and their effect on the Australian economy.

After the Depression of the 1890s, Australia's strategy to recover its economic base was to diversify its industries, to seek new trading partners, and to open new markets for its products. The Proclamation of Federation in 1901, which abolished tariffs between the states and created an Australian common market, and the period of world peace that preceded 1914 both assisted in the diversification of the nation's economy. A revival in the export of primary products, before the mainstay of Australian export trade, was joined by expansion in domestic manufacturing industries. Australia developed markets in western Europe and to a lesser extent in Asia while its trade with Britain declined after the United Kingdom introduced a preferential tariff in Britain's favour in Australia in 1906. As a result of the national plan to economic recovery, by 1914 Australia had broadened its pattern of trade so that it was less dependent on its international trading partner, Britain, and it had again become attractive for investment from overseas. But this welcome return to relative prosperity was soon to be upset by the declaration of war.[3]

With the onset of World War I it was a forgone conclusion in Australia that, as a member of the British Empire, the people would support the "mother" country in the struggle against the aggressor, Germany. Parliament immediately offered to send a contingent of 20,000 soldiers to any chosen destination, voted £100,000 to Belgium and granted the executive widespread powers under the *War Precautions Act 1914*. Enlistments began at once, and enthusiastic volunteers – motivated by the prospect of pay, travel, and adventure – flocked to recruiting centres to enlist in the new contingent to be known as the Australian Imperial Force (AIF).[4]

In Europe, however, Germany flowed down through Belgium and into France during the latter part of 1914, and it became clear that there would be no quick victory for Britain and her Allied forces. In Australia, the closure of European markets, shortage of shipping, and uncertainty about the future brought a serious disruption in the economy and severely hindered Australia's export industry. Added to these hardships, drought conditions over most of the agricultural districts at home culminated in a huge reduction of the wheat harvest compared to that of the previous year and many men were thrown out of work. During 1914 the rate of unemployment increased from 5.9% to 11%.[5]

The people of Norfolk Island joined the move to support Britain in the European conflict. In the first year of World War I, 25 men from Norfolk Island enlisted in the Commonwealth forces, two of whom were killed at the Dardanelles, and four wounded. By the end of the war a total of 78 men had volunteered to serve with the Australian and New Zealand imperial forces. Twelve men had been killed and twelve wounded or incapacitated; awards for bravery were given to five of their number. Anxious to support their soldiers during the war, the people raised a total of £1,580 towards the war effort through the activities of eleven patriotic funds – a generous contribution for a population of only about 850 people.

A tribute to the island's veterans who served during the war was "solemnly observed" eleven years after the Armistice at a combined religious service on Anzac Day 1929. A historic ceremony was held at which Acting Administrator H S Edgar JP unveiled a "dignified memorial" in commemoration of the veterans' war service. This was the end result of a resolution carried at a public meeting on 17 January 1919:

> that in the opinion of this meeting it is due to our boys who enlisted to serve King and country, that a fitting memorial be erected to their honour.[6]

Soon after the start of the war a parliamentary party of nine politicians, accompanied by J A Carrodus, a departmental officer, made an official visit to Norfolk Island to foster goodwill and to see Australia's new territory. The party of two senators, Senators McDougall and Blakey, and seven members of parliament, Messrs Catts, West, Matthews, Anstey, W Johnston, Piggot, and Palmer, spent three weeks on the island before returning to Sydney via Lord Howe Island on 20 January 1915. Frequent informal meetings were held and various social events arranged. A public meeting was held on 12 January at which the Islanders raised a number of matters of concern. Some of these related to the high cost of the administration as well as the people's desire to return to a fully elected council. Contentious old issues resurfaced, such as ownership of the island and houses and the people's objection to the requirement that they sign a lease before permission could be given to occupy the houses.

Henry Menges, a German resident of many years, broached an issue that was to become a significant grievance and the subject of vigorous debate. He complained about the anomalous situation that existed in Murphy's dual role, in that he was both the administrator and chief magistrate. The community's objection to this situation remained a point of contention until the *Norfolk Island Act* was amended in 1935. In his subsequent report to the minister, Carrodus stated the party had been warmly welcomed and their care successfully arranged, but there had been so many complaints at the public meeting that it had not been possible to hear them all; but he added this was "usual" when a parliamentary visit was made to a new territory.

Murphy, however, had been disturbed by proceedings at the meeting, and he wrote a long letter to Hunt on 5 February 1915 indicating that he wished to present further information and clarify certain matters that had been raised, as there had not been time for him to read the meeting minutes Carrodus wrote before they were sent to the department. Murphy informed Hunt about the "dominating influence Charles Nobbs wielded at Executive Council meetings". While Nobbs initially took a positive view of the transfer to the Commonwealth, this approval had not been extended to Murphy. It was "the same old story over and over again", Murphy wrote, "when anyone . . . vested with any authority visited the island, the same old tales of woe [were] poured out". Using his persuasive power with many in the community, Nobbs "pumped a lot of gratuitous information into the sympathetic ears" of some council members who tended to take him seriously, and he managed to gain their support. Some of the charges made were objections to Murphy's salary, which, in Nobbs's opinion, was "excessive", and Murphy's duties, he declared only amounted to answering about a couple of letters a month and a secretary was "altogether unnecessary etc".

With regard to the demand for a totally elected council,

Murphy's letter recalled that this had been given a "fair trial and found to be defective", and since public work was then paid out of the island's appropriation, it was necessary that at least half of the council should be nominated by the government. Murphy thought that Carrodus might have misunderstood his remarks about the proposed new council at the meeting.

Referring to Henry Menges, Murphy pointed out that he "talked a lot of rubbish" when he declared that he had heard the chief magistrate "discussing case after case" before sitting on the bench. Reflecting on Menges's attack on the administration and British justice, Murphy thought his opinion might have been influenced by the current war in Europe. A number of other issues brought up during the visit were included in the letter.

During debates in the House of Representatives on 2 and 10 June 1915, one of the visitors, J H Catts, member for Cook, reported to members of what he saw as the current state of affairs on the island. He damned the government's treatment of the Islanders in regard to their eviction from the houses and criticised the high cost of £3,000 allotted to the administration for the government of only 150 families. The number of positions – the administrator and his secretary, a customs officer and medical officer, as well as a postmaster, secretary to the executive council and a policeman with two assistants – Catts considered was a "gross extravagance" and he contended that "one Administrator and a policeman could do all the work necessary for the 600 people on the Island". Referring to the executive council of seven members, only two of whom were elected by the people, Catts stated that the council had practically no authority in their government and that the people ought to have the right to manage their own local affairs. About the public meeting, he stated "there was more ability manifested by the Islanders than is found in most municipal bodies" in Australia and that it was a "farce" to employ so many government men for so few people.[7]

Another of the visitors, A C Palmer, member for Echuca, saw the "vexed question" of the administration in different terms. He noted that the residents of the island believed that they should have a much larger share in government than they presently held and they claimed "complete autonomy"; but, Palmer acknowledged, the Commonwealth could not meet that claim. It was, on the other hand, "incumbent" upon the government to give the Islanders "considerable measure of redress". This could be achieved by adopting Atlee Hunt's recommendation of 1914 for an executive council of twelve members, six to be elected and six to be nominees. Palmer thought that this scheme would "satisfy" the residents, "especially if they were given the preponderance of representation", and it would work towards the island becoming a self-supporting economy in the future. He remarked that he had formed a "high opinion" of Murphy as administrator: "he [was] the right man in the right place". Murphy had inaugurated work on a system of experimental farm plots with the expectation that this innovation would provide farmers with practical assistance. His aim was to stimulate activity among the settlers to create worthwhile opportunities for future industry and agriculture.[8]

A *Sydney Morning Herald* article on 22 June 1915 reported on the success of the parliamentary visit and praised Murphy as being a well-liked and competent head of the island government. No mention was made in the article of any dissent at the public meetings. Even the adverse critic J H Catts had admitted in the House that he was "impressed" by Murphy as being a "very capable Administrator". In contrast to Murphy's letter about the meeting, the impression conveyed to the general public in Australia about the state of affairs on Norfolk Island was somewhat benign.[9]

Soon after the above debate, the sought-after change in the constitution of the executive council was achieved. It was recorded in the *Annual Report* to the minister for external affairs that from 14 July 1915 the executive council law was amended to provide for twelve councillors, six of whom were to be appointed by the administrator and six elected by the people. As before, the council was to have control of public work, such as the care, construction, and management of the public roads and certain public works, as well as other duties.

At the end of the island's first year as a territory of Australia, the administrator reported that there was a marked improvement in the value of the island's exports. The amount had increased from £1,193 in 1914 to £40,000 for the year ended 30 June 1915. The disparity between exports and imports, however, remained; the imports amounting to £12,119. The principal exports were lemon juice, passionfruit pulp, coffee, oranges, lemon seeds, potatoes, onions, hides, horsehair, wool, and a small quantity of arrowroot. Occasionally horses and poultry were shipped to the South Sea Islands.

During the year a new company, Pacific Fisheries and Trading Company, had been formed to provide a supply of fish for export, smoked or frozen. It was thought that this company would benefit the island by creating a local market for its produce for which cash would be paid. The company invested in the erection of a freezing chamber, and it was building a smokehouse, with other requirements, at a total cost of around £1,000. In addition to fish, the company intended to purchase local fruit, coffee, poultry, and other produce that Murphy thought would encourage cultivation and local industry generally. Several small factories had been established in conjunction with the lemon industry, but the shortage of funds made launching the products on the open market difficult; on the other hand, the removal of the duties on Norfolk Island products greatly assisted these developments. At the end of the first financial year Murphy stated:

> On the whole, the outlook is brighter, and greater facilities for commercial expansion have been provided since the Island was accepted by the Commonwealth of Australia.

At this time the general expectation that Norfolk's economy would rapidly expand seemed possible.[10]

For the next two years improvements continued, but in 1918 a downward trend began. Murphy noted that shipping accommodation was restricted to half the usual amount as a result of the international crisis, and this was reflected in the decrease in exports. As industries based their operations on a monthly steam service, when the number of ships available were reduced by half, the factory output declined accordingly. The main industries, lemons and fish, were affected by falling prices and the Pacific Fisheries and Trading Company which had inspired such optimism was forced to suspend operations. The administrator concluded his report by reiterating the need for improvement in transport facilities.[11]

By 1919 the impact of World War I was still being felt by the island community. There were a number of cases of pneumonic influenza, industrial disturbances in Australia, and a general depression in trade, attributable to the war. All of this resulted in a further decline in exports and an increase in imports that was to a large extent due to increased prices of goods generally. No fish was exported that year and it seemed doubtful that the fishing company would renew its operations, but as the war was by that time over, Murphy hoped that industry would recover and the economy improve.[12]

Around this time a change occurred that significantly affected the population of the island and its future development. The authorities of the Melanesian Mission announced that they were planning to move their headquarters further north to the Solomon Islands. They left Norfolk Island in 1920. Extensive discussions and negotiations were required to accomplish the move, during which a good deal of legal advice and opinion was sought. This process began in 1919, but it was not finally achieved for another 23 years, when the Church of England Lands Ordinance 1937–1942 was passed.

Murphy's confidence in 1919 that the economy would improve after the war when commerce gradually recovered its momentum was, unhappily, not realised. In 1922 Administrator J W Parnell reported a great falling-off in both exports and imports. The abundant crop of lemons proved to be of very little value to growers and the inhabitants generally. Shipments of potatoes and onions for the Sydney market brought poor returns, and in a few instances debit notes were received. As a result of the small figure for exports, there was a considerable decrease in custom duties collections.

This pattern of low returns on exports continued until around 1926, when Acting Administrator Murphy was able to report a reversal of the downward trend with a slight increase in the figures for exports. Murphy had returned to the island at the request of the Commonwealth Government following a decision to hold a royal commission on Norfolk Island affairs.

Colonel E T Leane, appointed administrator and chief magistrate on 1 July 1924, arrived on the island a week later on 7 July. He was absent from Norfolk for a period of six months in 1925 due to his appointment as deputy administrator of the Northern Territory during the absence of the administrator, F C Urquhart. Dr A S Patton functioned as acting administrator and acting chief magistrate during Leane's absence.[13]

Leane's short term on Norfolk Island was fraught with controversy and discontent. By his superior demeanour and lack of tact in dealing with the community, he made himself grossly unpopular. Evidence of the general dissatisfaction felt by the community was apparent in the many complaints made against his actions as administrator. There was, in addition, "convincing testimony" from a number of witnesses that statements made by Mrs Leane caused much dissatisfaction in the social life of the community.[14]

In his only *Annual Report* (1925) Leane made a statement referring to the "original Pitcairners" about which the Islanders were acutely aggrieved. He wrote that there had been a "great deal of romance" written about the people, so that they had come "to regard themselves as a special race, whose right it [was] to be cared for by others, without any obligation on their part to others". It was in this atmosphere of extreme tension that the royal commission began hearing evidence.[15]

Colonel Leane and the royal commission

By letters patent dated 20 January 1926, the governor-general of the Commonwealth of Australia commissioned Francis Whysall, Esq, to:

> to enquire into and report upon the system of administration in force in and in connection with the Territory of Norfolk Island and to investigate any complaints by residents of the Territory in regard to local conditions with a view to the suggestion of such remedial measures as may appear desirable.

Evidence was received in Sydney over three days in January that year and later on Norfolk Island. Whysall arrived on the island on 2 February 1926. He first familiarised himself with the geography of the island, the residents, their pursuits, and the local conditions, then, on 8 February, his commission was read to a large gathering of the inhabitants assembled at the courthouse. The scope and method of enquiry was explained and an announcement made that the services of the commission's secretary would be available to any resident who might experience difficulty in the presentation of evidence on any matter; many residents took advantage of this offer during the proceedings. The settlers raised a large number of issues to which Whysall gave full consideration and a summary of his observations and suggestions that, he hoped, might ameliorate the conflict.

By a resolution of the island's executive council, a public meeting was convened on 9 February. C C R Nobbs, councillor, was deputed to place evidence before the commission in relation to administrative and other matters, the conditions of which were considered disadvantageous to the Islanders. A large number of issues were raised.

Ninety-seven witnesses were examined, and 183 exhibits – chiefly documentary in character – were tendered over the weeks to 30 April 1926 when Commissioner Whysall left the territory. The report of the commission disclosed a "disturbed state of the public mind", mainly due to a loss of public confidence in the system of administration of justice, and particularly in the present administrator as chief magistrate. There were problems with landing places, the steamship service, land, and several other matters, all of which contributed to the social unrest felt by the community and ascribed in evidence to the actions and attitude of the administrator, Colonel E T Leane and his wife. Whysall began by outlining details of the system of administration provided under the *Norfolk Island Act* (No. 15 of 1913). As stated earlier, control of the island was vested in the Governor-General of the Commonwealth of Australia, and executive government of the territory was vested in the resident administrator, who also acted as chief magistrate. The administrator was under the "immediate direction" of the minister for home and territories. In the use of his authority the administrator was required to "exercise a general supervision over the affairs of the Island"; he was "accountable for the enforcement of obedience to the laws" of the territory and the "proper exercise of other functions" prescribed by the *Norfolk Island Administration Law* (No. 2 of 1913).

Other information from the 1913 Act was stated regarding the laws, rules, and regulations already in force on the island, together with particulars of government positions and salaries and the annual Commonwealth grant. Commenting on the foregoing, Whysall stated that the:

> administrative policy of the Government [was] directed to the material, moral and social well-being of the inhabitants, special consideration being given to the improvement of facilities for trade and intercourse with the mainland and the interests of the original Islanders.

Finally he observed that:

> without detriment to the welfare of the inhabitants, no material alteration in the system of general administration [could] be recommended, nor can any substantial reduction in expenditure be suggested without serious curtailment of the benefits derived by the residents from the educational, medical, postal, bank, police and other services provided by the government.[16]

It was clear to the commissioner through the hearing that the current system of the administration of justice was the cause of much resentment and trouble in the minds of the community. The Norfolk Island Progress Association had been formed in response to members' dissatisfaction with the method and manner of justice administration that had been in force from 1914 where one person held the dual role of administrator and chief magistrate. This system meant that legal redress was not available to aggrieved parties in cases in which it was believed justice had miscarried. It was to this issue that Henry Menges alluded during the parliamentary visit in 1915.

Referring to a petition from the association to the minister for home and territories, the "ostensible purpose" of the petition, Whysall considered, was to attract attention to the alleged unsatisfactory system of justice and excessive expenditure. Its "underlying motive" was to obtain an investigation into matters dealt with by the Magistrates Court in its civil and criminal jurisdiction, and the amelioration of conditions relating to affairs of justice. It was contended in evidence generally that the present system, which admitted "partiality", was responsible for the miscarriage of justice in cases dealt with both by the administrator as chief magistrate, and a "recently appointed" justice, H S Edgar, JP, sitting alone.[17]

Whysall made a number of suggestions with regard to the system of administration. The first recommended that provision be made by an amending ordinance for the appointment of justices of the peace with the necessary powers, authorities, privileges, and immunities enabling any two justices sitting with the chief magistrate as chairman of such bench of magistrates to hear and determine by majority within the civil or criminal jurisdiction of the court, "excepting cases above the amount or value of £20". The next suggested that four reputable Norfolk Island residents could be appointed to the Commission of the Peace in equal numbers of original Islanders or their descendants and others who had acquired an interest in the territory. Whysall thought the Administration Law 1913 should be amended by provision of a further right of appeal to the governor-general against the judgement or order of the Magistrates Court in its civil or probate jurisdiction in respect of any sum or matter at issue or respecting any property or civil right above the amount or value of £20", within a limited time and payment of a fee of £1.

A right of appeal to the governor-general could, similarly, be made "against a verdict or judgement of the Magistrates Court in all offences against the criminal laws in force within the Territory where such right of appeal is not prescribed in the 'Appeals Ordinance 1919' ". Finally, that provision could be made in the proposed Amending Appeals Ordinance "for regulating such appeals and the proceedings in, relating to, and consequent on such appeals".[18]

Exception was taken to the constitution of the executive council at the public meeting in February. A resolution was carried that provided for the council to be "wholly elected" and that the administrator "should not be ex officio-member". One of the principal reasons for the proposed change was that it was felt that the six appointed members were not representative of the residents. C C R Nobbs had noticed that on many occasions when he was present at meetings the six appointed members were "under the impression that they were under an obligation to vote for what was termed the Government". If all members were elected there would be no suggestion of bias in their votes.

With respect to the administrator being an ex-officio member at council meetings, evidence taken suggested that members would feel "much freer" to discuss matters when the administrator was not present. Nobbs also expressed the opinion that the "powers of the Executive Council should be extended and all proposed ordinances submitted to it and the decision of the council, whether for or against, acted upon accordingly". Opinions differed about Nobbs's proposals.

The administrator was glad to note that the council was not "blindly" following Nobbs's lead.[19]

As part of his evidence, Nobbs made reference to an offensive remark that had been uttered by Leane in response to certain proceedings that took place during a council meeting. It was alleged that Leane said "I may tell you whether you are in favour of it or not. It is going to be." The people were highly incensed and they considered this comment to be an affront to their dignity and a measure of Leane's arrogance and lack of tact.

During the hearing of this evidence, the administrator stated that "it is my opinion the Executive Council is futile", and he recommended that "serious consideration be given to its abolishment, and replacement by some other form of responsibility for the utilisation of what should be a valuable form of taxation, and to cope with the manifest necessity to prevent the spread of noxious weed . . . ".[20]

Leane's later letter to the Secretary of the Home and Territories Department, dated 14 May 1926, described Nobbs as a reactionary and stated that the council was a "menace to the future prosperity of the Island". He urged the minister to pass an ordinance for the purpose of abolishing the council as it was then constituted before the date of the next election and, presumably, replacing it with one more amenable to negotiation with the administration.[21]

In his "observations" Whysall wrote that the selection of competent members for the council should be "carefully exercised". The work entrusted to it had been sadly mismanaged in the past and a "means to correct this and ensure more satisfactory results [would be] difficult to find". He noted that further suggestions to assist this situation were made under other headings in his report, for example, noxious weeds, public works, and depasturage. It was felt that Whysall's suggestions would be appreciated and implemented by the council; and "thus the end in view would be accomplished".[22]

The evidence in relation to land matters was dealt with in three parts: the claim of the original Pitcairners and their descendants; anomalies and difficulties associated with the land; and difficulties with the administration of estates. In Part I the commissioner considered it was not necessary to deal exhaustively with the subject of claims made by the original Pitcairners then living on the island, as this question had been reviewed a number of times in the past. He did, however, deem it advisable to present the evidence submitted by Henry Menges that the "definite promises of the authorities that Norfolk Island should be the absolute property of the Pitcairners and their descendants had not been honoured". Extracts from parliamentary papers dealing with the transfer in 1856 were advanced in support of this claim. Witnesses, including C C R Nobbs and Cornelius Quintal, an original Pitcairner, claimed that the government had "departed" from the promises originally made at the time of the transfer.

During the proceedings Whysall reminded the people that the letter of 5 July 1854 from B Toup Nicolas, as again submitted, denied the Pitcairners' claim to "possessory rights in the whole of the land at Norfolk Island"; and it noted that the decision of the authorities had been conveyed to the petitioners at that time. The complainants presently claimed that the "reason for the apparent change of Government policy" in land matters and its connection with certain houses that had been in the possession of the Islanders for a number of years after arrival at the island was "never . . . stated to the satisfaction of the Islanders concerned". The legal opinion received on this point from F M Bladen, RRGS, barrister-at-law and librarian, who had recently collected all the data regarding the transfer of the settlers to Norfolk Island, said "that the Islanders have no good, legal backing for their claim to possessory rights in the soil of the whole of Norfolk Island is unquestionable". Whysall's observations recorded that "the rights of the Crown in Norfolk Island were decided many years ago" and the decision communicated to the petitioners. The current representations made to the commission were "briefly dealt with in order that the inhabitants might become fully acquainted with the facts. This should make the position clear to the Islanders, and remove what had been advanced as a factor in the unrest in evidence at the present time".

Part II referred to the resolution made at the public meeting on 9 February 1926 that stated "land matters should be thoroughly investigated and any anomalies set right". A number of cases in relation to particular lots selected under the "Carrington" system were presented and the commissioner's observations and recommendations made.

Administration of deceased estates was another problem submitted in Part III. Examples of six estates were used and the circumstances of each outlined. After consideration, Whysall's opinion was again stated in his observations and suggestions were made.[23]

Another two subjects of importance to the island's economy – agriculture and industries – were included in the report. In commenting about the state of agriculture on the island,

Whysall reminded the commission that in recent years the Melanesian Mission had vacated several blocks of land that had been taken up under leasehold conditions extending over 28 years by people from Australia, who appeared to be eager to make the best use of the fertile soils. Other settlers had been encouraged by the example of the mainlanders and were spurred on to increased efforts in clearing of land and raising crops, particularly bananas, for which there was a good market in Australia.

Colonel Leane had been active in his endeavours to demonstrate methods of raising crops and increasing production with only "ordinary effort". A photograph of a portion of wasteland that he had turned into a productive vegetable garden was shown to illustrate what could be achieved. Through correspondence and experiments, Leane attempted, with the cooperation of the Islanders, to assess the value of using artificial manure. He was, however, disappointed in the lack of interest shown by the farmers to whom he had distributed manure for "trial purposes". This experiment had only limited success.

Whysall found that the "come-day, go-day" attitude many of the Islanders had to effort in agricultural production was unfortunate, but he hoped that the example recently set by some of the Islanders would inspire other farmers to take advantage of the possibilities for production.

Four industries mentioned under this heading were lemon juice and peel, passionfruit pulp, dairying, and whaling. The commissioner was doubtful that the formerly remunerative lemon juice and peel industry could be revived, as competition from the growing citrus industry in New South Wales was able to adequately supply the market in Australia. The passionfruit that grew wild practically all over the island was of "excellent" quality and compared favourably with the best grown in Australia. In 1925 the crop exported was valued at £220. The dairying industry was in difficulties. There had been a low yield of butter in 1924 and an even lower yield the following year. Some residents had commented that butter-making was not profitable at certain times in the year and that it was cheaper to import butter than it was to produce it. The report stated that, aside from this, the yield was "absurdly low" and that it was "most locally attributable to the poor quality of the herds", as recorded elsewhere in the report. "With a better class of stock" and "more rigid supervision" it was felt that the butter yield should improve considerably; and the manufacture of cheese could also be undertaken.

The whaling industry had been in abeyance during the past two years. There was, apparently, some difficulty in placing a previous yield of oil and in the absence of quick financial returns the boatmen had "slackened" in their pursuit of whales. The wreck of a motor launch destined for the island had been a serious setback for the industry, but it was hoped with the aid of "up to date plant" the industry could be revived and prove profitable to whalers and beneficial to the island. [24]

At the end of the commission Whysall addressed what, in his opinion, was the reason for the social unrest within the community. Following on from his ideas in the introduction to the report, he stated that it was "regrettable" to record that he concurred with the "convincing testimony" of a number of the witnesses with regard to statements made by Mrs Leane which were, he found, the cause of widespread dissatisfaction in the social life of the island. The promise Leane made in public at the swearing-in ceremony – that he would resign his commission if within six months the people were not satisfied with his performance as administrator – was not honoured by him and the people were angry.

In his evidence Leane sought to justify his attitude towards the community by recounting a great deal of scandal concerning the people that may or may not have been true. It was, however, "incomprehensible" that as a "responsible" representative of government he should, without confirmation, have given credence to and acted upon such statements which "in their application to the people generally, had no foundation in fact".

From evidence heard during the proceedings, it was clear to the commissioner that the Islanders looked to the administrator for the:

> maintenance of a dignity appropriate to his office but it [was] contended that an attitude autocratic and superior in its character, associated with elaborate formal arrangements for the attendance of an administrative party at public functions [was] alien to the conditions of the territory and the simple lives of its people.

It was, on the other hand, to Leane's credit that he had carried out excellent work in the rehabilitation of public buildings; and his initiative to reafforest the island, to improve methods in agriculture, and to establish favourable markets for island produce and other proposals were to be commended.

In conclusion, the commissioner found that the "widely divergent views" between the administrator and the people made "healthy cooperation" impossible, and that, for this reason, the:

> interests of the Commonwealth and of Norfolk Island would best be served by the immediate withdrawal of the present Administrator in favour of one possessed of proved temperamental suitability and a knowledge of community oversight and management.[25]

While Leane had some supporters among the residents, the overwhelming majority of settlers were angry and disillusioned, and they were glad to see him leave on 31 May 1926. Soon after, on 12 August, M V Murphy arrived at the island for the second time as a government representative, to take up the post of acting administrator and acting chief magistrate.[26]

At the end of the year the *Annual Report* for 1926 stated that exports had increased from those of the previous year but so had imports. Nevertheless, the produce of the island had been shipped regularly and mainly "satisfactory" prices were received. Some very high prices had been paid for exports of bananas, and the future of the industry looked promising. The crop of potatoes also brought a very good price in the market.[27]

The years to the end of 1929 continued to show optimistic results, and the statistics recorded an expansion in the volume of trade. In 1927 the administrator, Major General V C M Sellheim, reported that Norfolk Island was entering "an era of unexampled prosperity", the principal export being bananas, but other vegetables and fruit were a positive addition to the export figures. Mr Justice C E Herbert succeeded as administrator in 1928, following Sellheim's untimely death. He was pleased to report at the end of year that exports rose to the high sum of £19,254 from a total of £6,156 only received for exports three years earlier. The general outlook of the people appeared to be one of "hopefulness and confidence", he said, but the infrequency of the steamer service and lack of ventilation in the holds of vessels providing transport worked against a successful outcome. Herbert's term, unfortunately, also ended when he died in office on 1 May 1929.

Colonel A J Bennett followed Herbert as administrator in 1929. He reported that the increase in import figures for that year was due to an influx of motor vehicles, 28 of which had been imported over the last twelve months. This, of course, reflected the "continued prosperity of the Territory". Exports for 1929 rose to £33,027 from the previous year as the banana industry continued to expand. As a result of the growth in the economy, Bennett announced that the territory had "passed from the barter to the money stage of dealing", and that a trading bank was "essential". Representations were at that time being made through the Commonwealth Government to have banking facilities extended to the island, as this would materially assist developments.

By 1929 the population had increased to 932 settlers. The *Annual Report* recorded that of the 6,694 acres of land held, about 4,522 acres of land were freehold and 2,171 acres of land were leasehold (around 2710, 1830, and 1880 hectares respectively). Most of the freehold land was held by the Norfolk Islanders and mainly comprised early grants made to the Pitcairners. At the end of Bennett's second year as administrator, it was evident that the social life of the community was undergoing a change that, it was thought, would be to the advantage of the people. The *Annual Report* for 1930 noted that of the nine marriages registered during the year, six were between Islanders and mainlanders. It was "interesting" to note that there was a "marked tendency" on the part of the Islanders, men and women, to marry mainlanders, and Bennett believed that future generations would be "more virile" as a result. It was also apparent that the former lack of incentive to work had given way to industry and the "intelligent application" thereof with the recent growth in the banana industry.

The extraordinary boom in the export of bananas over the latter years of the 1920s, on the other hand, did not continue during 1930. The years of prosperity were cut short by the effects of the Great Depression on the international economy. Trading for that year indicated a "marked decline" from 33% to 18% in trade with New Zealand. The irregular trips of the New Zealand government vessel GMV *Maui Pomare* finally ended with a discontinuance of the service in March 1930. The reason for the downturn on Norfolk, Bennett considered, was the reduction in the tourist traffic that existed "almost entirely" with New Zealand, and this was a matter for "grave concern".

The tourism trade with Australia had never been great, but with the current failing economy on the mainland there was no hope of financial assistance to fund improvements to landing places, or other public works, from that source. Ministerial approval had been given to open a further 130 acres (around 53 hectares) of Crown land for settlement, but it was of the "poorest grade" and may not have been productive. In agriculture, Bennett surmised that the "phenomenal" yield of bananas had apparently "lulled" planters into believing that fertiliser was not necessary, resulting in a poor yield. To make matters worse, it was the only crop grown specifically for export, so the recently discovered banana leaf spot disease which had spread rapidly through the plantations was the cause of great alarm to growers.

Commenting on the cost of living on the island, Bennett noted that freeholders working on their own properties required comparatively little cash, as did leaseholders that paid the old nominal rent. New settlers, on the other hand, paid comparatively high rents and had to provide capital and support themselves until an income could accrue. Conditions on Norfolk Island at the end of the financial year presaged a severe economic decline with global repercussions.[28]

There were no improvements in the economy for 1931. The comparative statistics for imports and exports for the year indicated a recurrent high sum in the cost of imports and a sudden drop by nearly half in the income from exports for the year to 30 June 1931. It was seen that this "adverse trade balance" between imports and exports was "serious": the territory had felt the effect of worldwide depression.[29]

The new administrator, Captain Charles R Pinney, arrived at Norfolk Island on 18 July 1932. The population had increased to 1,074 persons, and the commencement of a passenger service with New Zealand via the SS *Morinda* augured well for an increase in tourism. But the number of visitors did not meet expectations and many planters left the island at that stage. Despite the "exceptionally unfavourable year", Pinney remarked that the planters had shown considerable "resourcefulness" in their endeavours to grow alternative crops and to find suitable markets for them.[30]

One year later, Pinney described the year to 30 June 1933 as the hardest year in the commercial history of the island. The New Zealand Government delivered a serious blow to the island economy by restricting the importation of bananas into the Dominion, and then by including the territory in its embargo on Australian fruit and vegetables. This embargo led to the withdrawal of the SS *Morinda* from the Auckland trade. Severance of communications with Auckland, Pinney wrote, represented a heavy loss to producers and the tourism trade. Other disappointments were mentioned in the report: expectations placed in the value of the Canadian Wonder bean crop did not eventuate, largely due to a serious outbreak of bean weevil; and about a third less bananas were shipped during the year as a result of New Zealand's restrictions. Although slight encouragement was given to the tourism trade by the visit of the RMS *Strathaird* and the 1,000 passengers who disembarked while the ship was at anchor, the ship only stayed twelve hours before departing with the visitors. Pinney did not see much hope for improvement in the economy while the Dominion embargo remained in force. There was "no prospect of remediation from that direction", but he praised the way in which all the settlers dealt with difficulties over the past two years; this, he recorded, "prevented an undue feeling of pessimism for the future of the Territory".[31]

A further decrease in the volume of trade followed in 1934, and Pinney declared the year to be "the most difficult period in the Island's history"; the conditions were "serious and becoming worse". The loss of the New Zealand market and poor prices for produce sent to the Sydney market meant that returns were "barely sufficient to provide planters with the necessities of life". The Chamber of Commerce, Planters Association, and Tourist Bureau were each doing their utmost to improve present conditions, but they found it hard to be optimistic.[32]

Despite the years of hardship over the early 1930s, the people appear to have pulled together at this time of crisis, but in 1934 and 1935 a number of contentious issues surfaced that led to significant changes in the Constitution. Internal struggles occurred in 1934 when community anxiety appeared to grow to such proportions that personal feelings were brought into council matters and the "Christian spirit" of goodwill and harmony among members seemed absent.

The first upset arose when C C R Nobbs sent a memorandum to the administrator that the council judged to be "discourteous and disrespectful". The official and verbatim minutes for 4 January 1934, at which the administrator was present, suggest the trouble arose over a letter from the private secretary to the council with the information that "His Honour" the administrator required an explanation of the irregularity in payments referred to in the council's letter No 79233 of 12 December 1933 to be supplied in writing for the Commonwealth Audit Officer on his next visit to the territory. The next day the private secretary forwarded a copy of a letter received from the president (Nobbs) of the executive council in an envelope addressed to "The Administrator, Norfolk Island", that "His Honour" considered both "disrespectful and unsatisfactory" and, as a result, this correspondence was to be drawn to the attention of the minister.

Members of the executive council were duly shocked by this

demonstration of unacceptable behaviour and Councillor A E Martin proposed:

> That this Council strongly disapproves of this discourteous memo, which purports to be an explanation of the Auditor's query re payments made to workmen addressed by the President to His Honour, the Administrator. It considers that the President has not carried out the wishes of the Council as no attempt at any explanation has been made, and as it also considers that a reflection has been cast on the Council as a whole by this very disrespectful memo it no longer has any confidence in him as President, and calls upon him to resign.

The president then gave a "lengthy explanation" in which he referred to a resolution passed by the council at the meeting of 4 October 1933. This meeting authorised Nobbs to organise public work gangs for the eradication of noxious weeds. This was done, and on completion of the work, Nobbs told the foreman to send the men to him for payment. Nobbs paid each man from his safe and obtained a receipt, and at a later date they were again paid in cash on their bills. He then presented the signed vouchers to the secretary of the council and the amount was drawn from the Commonwealth Savings Bank, the president and the secretary having the authority to draw on that account. Nobbs claimed that there was no vestige of irregularity on his part and that he knew of no law or by-law that had been violated by his actions. He concluded by "reminding" the councillors that he was an elected member and that there was "no procedure whereby he [could be] removed" from office. At the request of the majority of the council members, Councillor Martin put the motion to the meeting. The motion was carried by ten votes to two.

The next day Nobbs advised the minister by cable that an "impossible situation" had arisen in council between himself as president, the administrator in his role as chairman and the council members. Nobbs contended that the resolution passed against him was "ultra vires" and he "respectfully" submitted that the situation demanded a "full enquiry by a competent, impartial person as peace, order and good government was impossible under existing conditions". Nobbs was correct in his knowledge of the law as the council was informed on 12 January 1934 that a reply had been received by "His Honour the Administrator", relative to the resolution of 4 January. The reply stated that there was "no apparent authority in law for the removal of the president of the Executive Council, and that the election of president can only be made pursuant to the Executive Council Ordinance". The council was not put off by this hindrance to their plan; members promptly passed a resolution to amend the Executive Council Ordinance 1925 to make provision for the removal of a president.

This was subsequently affirmed on 2 May 1934 when Ordinance No. 4 of 1934 amended the Executive Council Ordinance 1925, Section 3(3) to read:

> The office of President of the Council shall be vacated if at any meeting of the Council at least two-thirds of all the members of the Council elected or appointed by the Administrator vote in favour of the removal of the President from office.

At a special meeting of the executive council on 19 May 1934, when the administrator was in the chair, Pinney announced that a telegraphic communication had been received apparently in regard to the foregoing amendments. Nobbs protested that the meeting was not "a properly constituted meeting", that the document "purport[ed] to convey an amendment to the Ordinance" had been received by radio and was, therefore, not "proof" that it existed and had not been posted at the courthouse. Until that time he was still the president: "I am here by law, and until that law is amended to remove me I am here."

But the meeting was not to be diverted from its purpose:

> The foregoing resolution was read, the Chairman called for nominations for the office of President and Eustace Christian was elected President. Meanwhile, Nobbs left the Council chambers.

It is not possible to elicit a very clear picture of all that happened during this episode, but it seems that the very essence of the community's feeling and ethic of loyalty and respect for the authority of the Crown was damaged. Nobbs's behaviour that had caused widespread censure was in some quarters considered reprehensible.[33]

Two months later a petition, dated 31 July 1934, signed by a large number of residents was sent to the Governor-General of the Commonwealth of Australia in Canberra. The "loyal petitioners" of Norfolk Island requested that an inquiry be instituted into the "present intolerable conditions prevailing on [the] Island" and, they believed, a "drastic change" in the system of administration would restore normal conditions to the community. A list of nine grievances were stated, all of which had been aired before in one form or another. The first two issues were complaints about the "excessive and unwarranted powers" held by Pinney in his dual role as administrator and chief magistrate and those exercised by the collector of customs.

In his reply of 13 September 1934 to the Prime Minister's Department, Pinney pointed out that a minority of inhabitants had signed the petition. The statements made regarding the administrator and officials were "untrue" and they reflected the "state of hysteria" under which the people present laboured. Pinney concluded by suggesting that a visit from the minister in the near future would give "encouragement" to settlers whose outlook at that time was "nearly hopeless" and it may "tend to dispel many ancient grievances".

A short time before the July petition a public meeting had been held on 18 June 1934 for the purpose of considering the "advisability" of forming a "Norfolk Island Association" fully representative of all residents of the island. Views were expressed, and it was agreed that there was a need for action in a number of directions due to the present unsatisfactory state of business on the island.

Hostility towards the administrator and the collector of customs "intensified" when licences for the handling of cargo were granted to three persons other than the Norfolk Island Boating Company, apparently because the company had refused to unload the SS *Morinda*. Pinney had acted, however, in accordance with Customs Ordinance No. 7 of 1934 that required "all goods for import or export shall at Norfolk Island be conveyed to and from the ship only in boats licensed by the Administrator".[34]

The Norfolk Island Association protested about what they saw as "unfair" and "arbitrary" treatment meted out to the Norfolk Island Boating Company; and, as recommended by the executive council, the association requested that the Ordinance be repealed at the meeting of 6 September 1934. Councillor Lesley Quintal, referring to Customs Ordinance No. 7, drew members' attention to it as being the "cause of a great deal of unrest" on the island. After considerable discussion, a resolution was passed that this Ordinance be repealed and that it be replaced by a new ordinance. In the event, Ordinance No. 7 was not repealed, but another Ordinance, cited as "Licensing of Boats Ordinance 1934, No 14" was passed on 14 November 1934. This Ordinance gave the administrator sole power to issue licences for boats and boatmen engaged in lighterage activities. It clearly defined the terms and conditions under which licences could be granted, and it fixed penalties for any infringement of the regulations. Not surprisingly, the new legislation did not suit the Islanders, and it remained a contentious issue for a considerable length of time. No. 14 of 1934 was finally repealed on 14 September 1961 when the Lighterage Ordinance 1961 (No. 6) was notified in the *Norfolk Island Government Gazette*. It enabled the administrator to "establish, maintain and conduct a service, to be known as the Norfolk Island Lighterage Service, for the carriage of cargo and passengers to and from ships calling at Norfolk Island". The administrator, as a result, had full control of the lighterage service.

On the other hand, soon after Ordinance No. 14 of 1934 was passed, the administrator informed the government in a prime minister's minute, dated 14 January 1935, that the association was composed of all the "malcontents of the Territory" and it "espoused the cause of the Boating Company and that of Mr Macarthur-Onslow", an alcoholic, who was then under a threat of deportation for "activities subversive to law and order"; and he was not in favour of repeal of Ordinance No. 7.[35]

The administrator was requested to submit his opinion about the current situation on the island. Among other observations, he thought that "financial stress" had a "good deal" to do with the present unrest. Old grievances had led to an objective, adopted at the inaugural meeting of the association in June 1934, that they were "entitled to home rule". Pinney, anxious to "disabuse the residents" about the "current propaganda in support of self-government", again suggested that a visit from the minister might give encouragement to the settlers.[36]

In response to the social unrest, financial hardship, and Pinney's request, the Commonwealth Government authorised a visit to Norfolk Island in March 1935 by the minister in charge of territories, the Right Honourable Sir George Pearce KCVO, who was accompanied by his wife, and J R Halligan of the Prime Minister's Department, Canberra.

At a public meeting held on 20 March, the residents were given the opportunity to ventilate their complaints and state their case for administrative change. The minister received a number of deputations from representatives of all sections of the community and residents expressed their views, after which Pearce addressed the public meeting. He "intimated" that "owing to the depressed economic condition of the island, the Commonwealth Government had decided to make a grant of £2,000, to be spent on public works, thus placing more money in circulation in the Territory".

In addition to the grant, the minister announced that important changes would be made to the law covering the administration of the territory. Central to these was the abolition of the executive council of six appointed members and six elected members and its replacement with an advisory council of eight members elected by residents. Pearce thought that this would give the settlers greater opportunities for expressing their views in a constitutional manner through the council than had formerly been available to them.

At the same meeting a letter, dated 30 March 1935, from the administrator's office had been received by cable, and it was directed that it be read to council.

> As a result of the visit from the Minister for Territories to Norfolk Island, Commonwealth Government has decided to institute certain changes in form of Administration etc:- including firstly Administrator relinquishes position of Magistrate and arrangements to be made for appointment of local residents as Justices of the Peace to deal with minor criminal and civil cases and for Magistrate with wider jurisdiction visit Island deal with more serious cases. Secondly present Executive Council to be terminated and to be replaced by wholly elected Advisory Council, to advise on all matters affecting the island. No nominee members Council thirdly expenditure public monies to be carried out by Administrator, after consultation with Advisory Council. Franchise to remain as at present. Other details Advisory Council to be arranged by government later.

The minister desired to learn the views of the executive council regarding the foregoing proposals "as soon as possible". The administrator then retired to enable council to give full consideration to the foregoing.[37]

As a result of the proposals made by the minister to the Islanders at the public meeting, it was necessary to amend the *Norfolk Island Act 1913* to make provision for the establishment of an advisory council, as outlined at the meeting. The principal Act was amended and cited as *Norfolk Island Act 1913–1935* on 12 April 1935.

This Act foreshadowed Ordinance No. 10 of 1935, cited as Advisory Council Ordinance 1935 on 25 June 1935, the first of three ordinances necessary to enact the changes Pearce referred to at the March public meeting.

Apart from a wholly elected council, as described above, section 7 of the Advisory Council Ordinance 1935 provided for the subdivision of the island into four wards. Persons living in each ward would elect two of their number to represent them in the council, thus making a total of eight councillors to represent all the Islanders. Section 9 defined the qualifications for enrolment: "Every person resident on Norfolk Island, whether male or female" who was natural born or a naturalised British subject, and who was aged 21 years or more and had lived on the island for six months immediately preceding the date of application for enrolment, was entitled to enrol.

Section 12 provided that all persons entitled to vote and whose name was on the roll were required to vote; failure to do so incurred a penalty of £2. Section 13 covered the qualification necessary for the election of members. Any person that was entitled to vote at an election of members for any ward was eligible for election as a member for that or any other ward, provided that the person was not eligible for election as a member for more than one ward. This, therefore, meant that women were eligible to vote for the first time since 1896, and they could also be elected as a representative for their ward. By 1935, as a result of the new legislation, government authorities had recognised the rights of women and their contribution to the general well-being of the island's community.

The powers of the council were described in section 21 of the Ordinance:

1. The council could advise the administrator in relation to any matter affecting Norfolk Island, including the making of new ordinances or the repeal or amendment of existing ordinances;
2. All advice from the council was to be expressed in the form of a resolution;
3. If council had advised the administrator in relation to any matter, and the administrator failed to act, or acted otherwise than, in accordance with that advice, he should forward to the minister a memorandum setting out his reasons for failing so to act or for so acting;
4. Upon receipt from the council of any proposal for a new ordinance or regulation, or for the repeal or amendment of any existing law, ordinance, or regulation, the administrator should forward the proposal to the Minister, together with a memorandum setting out his views with respect to the proposal.

This Ordinance went part way to satisfy an earlier complaint made by C C R Nobbs, who sought a fully elected executive council, and it ensured that the council's proposal, would reach the minister, but it did not agree to Nobbs's 1926 request that: "The decision of Council whether for or against be acted upon accordingly" or the subsequent rumour, circulated by some, that the island should be granted "home rule".[38]

The second legislative change was associated with the administration of the territory. The *Administration Law 1913*, the principal ordinance, had been amended in 1922 and 1923. On 22 May 1935 another ordinance, cited as the Administration Ordinance 1935, was passed to make provision for a special magistrate and to define the powers of the chief magistrate: the Administration Ordinance (No. 2 of 1935) amended the principal Ordinance.

On 12 August 1936, the five preceding ordinances listed in the First Schedule of No. 40 of 1936 relating to the administration of Norfolk Island were repealed. There were a number of changes made and a new ordinance, No. 14, was to be cited as the Administration Ordinance 1936.

Ordinance No. 15 of 1936, the third of the seminal constitutional changes, established a court for the territory of Norfolk Island and for other purposes; this Ordinance was cited as the Judiciary Ordinance 1936 and it was promulgated on 16 December 1936. The old Magistrates Court, established by the Administration Law (No. 2 of 1913), was abolished and the Court of Norfolk Island was created. The jurisdiction of the court was divided into two parts: full and limited jurisdiction. When sitting in its full jurisdiction, it was constituted by a judge, the chief magistrate, or a special magistrate; and when sitting in its limited jurisdiction by a judge, the chief magistrate, a special magistrate, or by two or more justices of the peace.

The court sitting in its *limited* jurisdiction had jurisdiction to hear and determine all actions where the amount claimed was not more than £30, whether on a balance of account or otherwise; and jurisdiction to punish summarily all crimes and offences in respect of which a pecuniary penalty, or a sentence of imprisonment not exceeding six months, could be imposed. The court sitting in its *full* jurisdiction had jurisdiction to hear and determine all actions; to punish all crimes and offences; to grant probate and letters of administration; jurisdiction in all matters and cases whatsoever; and, subject to the Ordinance, to hear and determine appeals from any conviction of the court sitting in its limited jurisdiction. Finally, an appeal to the High Court of Australia from any judgement, order, decree, or sentence of the court, sitting in its full jurisdiction could be made.[39]

After the visit of Sir George Pearce and the announcement that a grant of £2,000 (to be distributed by the administrator) would be given to the Islanders for projects of public work, executive council meetings were held and a comprehensive list of works for upgrade was written. The majority of the settlers welcomed this financial assistance from the government for relief work, but perhaps inevitably, there was some discontent about the way in which the grant was spent. Council members passed a unanimous resolution indicating that the money had not been distributed in accordance with the scheme outlined by the minister. The administrator's reply assured the council that the method that had been followed "was discussed in detail with and approved by the Minister".[40] The next month another complaint arose that claimed "certain men" who had registered for relief work early had not been granted any work, while other men had been given "long periods of work"; and some single men with no dependents had been called out for a second time.

On the other hand, at the final meeting of the old executive council in July, the council passed a resolution headed "Expressions of Gratitude", in which they thanked the authorities in Canberra for their consideration over the past year, particularly with regard to assistance with road works, assisting leaseholders by the Crown Rents Ordinance 1934, reduction in the cost of gun licences, and a promise of assistance for "elderly residents in necessitous circumstances". The contrast between the complaints received by the administration and the gratitude given to it for benefits received by the Islanders might, perhaps, be explained by the fact that a relatively small number of residents had been politically active. Many residents were more hopeful than they had been that their situation might soon improve.[41]

The *Annual Report* for the year ended 30 June 1935 commented upon the troubles of the past year in that a "few persons" had resorted to political action as a "panacea for all the economic ills of the Territory". The economic situation was still "fraught with much difficulty", Pinney wrote, but he was optimistic that the "tide [was] slowly turning".

The first election for the newly constituted advisory council took place on 21 August 1935, and two representatives were elected for each of the four wards: Kingston, Cascade, Ball Bay, and Mount Pitt. One week later the first council meeting of the eight members elected their president. Two of the members nominated scored equal votes; the decision, therefore, was declared according to the law by lot, and C C R Nobbs was again elected to the post.

The advisory council continued to meet on a regular basis during the remainder of this period. Many issues came before the council, some of which caused a good deal of protest and debate. A list of resolutions passed by council during 1935 and 1936, however, which was accompanied by a summary of the action taken by the government in response to each matter, indicated that many of councils' requests were resolved with a positive outcome.[42]

Pinney's prediction in 1935 that the island economy would recover was accurate, as over the next few years the situation, despite some setbacks, showed a steady improvement. Several new settlers arrived to take up farming land, New Zealand lifted the embargo on citrus fruits, and there was an advance in trade in 1936. The following year some storm damage occurred, but Pinney reported that it had been a year of steady endeavour and progress. Recent financial assistance from government and the Commonwealth Bank had enabled industries to be developed, and this had led to a "marked improvement in the standard of living". Although there was an improvement in living conditions as a consequence of the increased flow of money in the economy, some settlers who had been trained as farmers and were inexperienced in marketing found difficulty in maintaining a reasonable living.[43]

Sir Charles Rosenthal, accompanied by Lady Rosenthal, arrived at Norfolk Island on 3 November 1937 to take over as administrator from Captain Pinney at the end of his term. There were setbacks in the year 1937–1938. Conditions of trade had been difficult and there were problems with agriculture.

There was a loss of income (£3,000) from the passionfruit and bean seed industries, but with advances received from the Commonwealth Government, special efforts were being made to establish them on a "permanent and remunerative basis".

In the next financial year, 1938–1939, drought conditions unfortunately resulted in the loss of many head of dairy cattle, but the Norfolk Island Cooperative Dairy Co Ltd continued to produce "excellent butter". Rosenthal also reported that a good result had been achieved with work on the roads, and the drainage of a large area of land near Kingston had been a result of an improved organisation of the public work gangs.

From the annual reports and a survey of the extensive amount of legislation that passed through council during this period, it seems that despite protest and heated discussion over some contentious issues, the great bulk of legislation proceeded into law without undue difficulty.

Aside from the annual grants provided by the Commonwealth Government for payment to the Norfolk Island Trust Fund to be used for the expenses of the administration, further grants were made during the 1930s. The initial grant of £2,000 for unemployment relief in 1935 was followed within a year by £2,000 for advances to settlers and £1,200 for cyclone damage repairs; £325 for distress relief was given at Christmas 1936, and two advances for the struggling passionfruit industry over 1937–1939 amounted to a total of £5,000.[44]

Population: growth, decline, and the economy

The state of the Norfolk Island economy can be seen in the

growth and decline of the population. From available population statistics for the period under review, the years of World War I to 1919 indicated an increase in the number of settlers from 800 rising to 883 in 1918 and then falling to 815 in 1919. The initial improvement in exports as a result of the island's transfer to the Commonwealth of Australia continued until 1918, when a general depression attributable to the war occurred and a downward trend followed.

The figures for 1920–1923 are not available, but in 1924 there was a further decline from 1919 to 726 settlers. The population remained less than 750 people up to 1926. Over these years exports decreased accordingly, probably as a result of the slow economic recovery after World War I and depressed market conditions, but in 1926 hopes were raised as the banana industry looked promising and good prices were obtained for the potato crop.

The population rose to 853 settlers in 1927; and exports increased by £7,422. There were further increases from 902 to 932 in 1929, as mainlanders arrived to take up land vacated by the Melanesian Mission and to take advantage of the current boom in agriculture.

Although there was still an increase to 942 people in 1930, including six new arrivals, trade with New Zealand declined by 18% and there was no regular shipping service. The increased population combined with the depleted resources therefore put a great strain on the economy and all community life. This situation was to continue until the end of 1935, when economic improvement seemed likely. As the population grew from 942 in 1930 to 1,161 settlers in 1935 together with the alarming decrease in exports during the Great Depression, the island economy was in a desperate state as, indeed, were the settlers themselves.

From 1933, however, when Pinney reported that there were equal numbers of Islanders and others, the number of departures from the island exceeded the number of new arrivals by 29 people. At the same time, New Zealand had placed an embargo on Australian fruit and vegetables, and thus added another problem to the already stretched economy.

The trend in the rate of departures continued from 1933 as settlers suffered from the losses incurred in the banana and other industries, even after trade began to improve in 1936 when New Zealand lifted the embargo on citrus fruit. Storm damage in 1937 exacerbated the rate of departures and 37 people left the island despite the expansion of trade in 1936–1937.

The population decreased to 983 in 1938 and 896 in 1939 as a result of further difficulties in trade, such as loss of income from the passionfruit and bean seed industries, as well as drought conditions; and departures for those years increased to 83 and 86 respectively. The likelihood of continual improvement in trade in 1936–1937 was, apparently, insufficient to stem the flow of departures to 1939.

Over this period the growth and decline of the population tended to lag behind the economic indicators of trade for the year, particularly in the early 1930s when the population grew steadily but the economy declined. Perhaps mainland settlers, already in deep economic distress, felt fertile Norfolk Island would offer more hope than could be expected under the present conditions in Australia.

The availability of the vacant Melanesian Mission land in 1920 enabled settlers from the mainland and elsewhere to take up land for farming purposes; immigrants gradually arrived, bringing new ideas and a fresh approach to the agricultural industry.

Chapter 5

World War II and Post-War Reconstruction: 1940 to 1965

When Britain and France declared war against Germany on 3 September 1939 the Australian national reaction was very different to that of 1914. As historian Russel Ward observed:

> There was no wild enthusiasm or false optimism – nor, for that matter, much sign of panic or profound fear.[1]

On the other hand, it was understood that Britain had declared war, and therefore, as Prime Minister Menzies announced, Australia was also at war.

Volunteers were enlisted in a second imperial force, vessels were assigned to the Royal Navy, and air squadrons trained in Canada were then sent to Britain. Although Britain and Germany waged war at sea, for the first eight months Britain and France refrained from any aggressive ground action in the west. Later dubbed the "phoney war", this period allowed the Allies valuable time to arm for battle. In 1940 two divisions of the second imperial force were posted to base camps in the British mandated territory of Palestine, ready to support Britain; however, for Australians the war seemed remote from home.[2]

The "phoney war" ended in Europe on 9 April 1940 when Germany invaded Denmark and Norway and full-scale land war engulfed most of Europe. Eighteen months later, hostilities began in the east on 7 December 1941. Japan bombed the American naval base at Pearl Harbor and simultaneously landed soldiers on the Malay Peninsula. The danger in the Pacific galvanised activity in Australia. Labor Prime Minister John Curtin declared war on Japan, and against strong opposition from the British prime minister, insisted that Australian troops in the Middle East be returned to defend their home country.[3] Australia, too, was inadequately prepared and vulnerable to attack; there was no mercantile fleet and only an emerging aircraft industry, but Australia's desperate efforts to defend the nation resulted in exceptional achievements in the manufacturing of munitions and other wartime industries during the war years in response to the emergency. Around the world countries opposed to Japan and Germany assessed their resources and developed appropriate strategies for defence. After Japan's entry into the war the Allies created a unified command in the south-west Pacific under the British General Sir Archibald Wavell, who took over what was known as the ABDA area – territories controlled by America, Britain, Holland (Dutch) and Australia – and Admiral Thomas C Hart of the United States Asiatic Fleet commanded all the naval forces. Wavell's command included Burma, Malaya, the Philippines, Netherlands East Indies, Dutch New Guinea, and later Northern Australia. Beyond this area east of the Philippines and Australia and New Zealand, the defence of the Pacific became the responsibility of the United States Navy.

In January 1942, in addition to the Pacific Ocean area, the Anzac area was created. It included east Australia, New Zealand, and part of New Guinea and was still the responsibility of the US Navy. Vice Admiral H F Leary was assigned to command the first Anzac Naval Force. When Singapore fell on 15 February 1941, the ABDA Command was dissolved and the strategic boundaries were changed into two spheres of influence. The Indian Ocean, including Burma, became the British sphere, and the Pacific Ocean including Australia and New Zealand fell to the United States.

The distance of over 9,500 kilometres between the main Allied bases in Australia and New Zealand and the United States ports of Pacific Ocean and a slightly less distance between the important subsidiary forward bases of Fiji, New Caledonia, and New Hebrides, meant that quick offensive action against Japan was not possible. Through early 1942 a series of mutually supporting island bases was built up through the Pacific, extending from the New Hebrides, where a huge naval base capable of undertaking heavy repair work on damaged ships was established at Havannah Harbour on Efate, to New Caledonia (the largest military and supply base), Fiji, Samoa, and Tonga.

By the end of March 1942 the division of the Pacific and the commands had been agreed. First, the south-west Pacific area under General Douglas MacArthur, with headquarters in Australia, included the Philippines, South China Sea, Netherlands East Indies (except Sumatra), the Solomon

Islands, Australia, and waters to the south. Second, the Pacific Ocean area under Admiral Chester Nimitz, Commander-in-Chief of the United States Pacific Fleet with headquarters at Pearl Harbor.

Nimitz's Pacific Ocean area was subdivided into three areas – northern, central, and southern – and it had joined MacArthur's command off the east coast of Australia. Most of the established Allied bases were in the southern Pacific area of more than 1.6 million square kilometres of ocean, dotted with groups of islands, and Nimitz commanded all Allied forces in that area, except the New Zealand land defences. Vice Admiral R L Ghormley, US Navy, was appointed his surrogate commander in the South Pacific in 1942, with headquarters in Auckland. Before the commands were finally settled, however, there were some differences of opinion between the army and navy during their negotiations. At this time, Australia and New Zealand "vigorously protested" against being placed in separate areas since they regarded both countries as a "strategical whole", but no consideration was given to this objection.[4]

Although the bulk of Australians had not been unduly perturbed by events in the west when war broke out, there were some politicians and government officials in the 1930s who were aware of Germany's swelling military strength in Europe, and Japan's ominous presence in the Pacific. In the late 1930s Menzies recognised the possible threat from the north "and the greatly strengthened Japanese forces arrayed menacingly", "poised for action" around the Pacific.[5]

On Norfolk Island, Administrator Rosenthal had also observed the build-up of Japanese armed forces. He realised that Norfolk Island's geographical position could make it a target for enemy attack, and he therefore approached the Department of Defence as early as 1938, pointing out the advantage of the island as an "observation zone" of strategic value. The department, however, replied that the establishment of an aerodrome on Norfolk Island at that time was "not essential".

The following year on 15 September 1939 Rosenthal again wrote to the Prime Minister's Department. In view of the war "just entered", he emphasised the wisdom of establishing an air force station at Norfolk Island, particularly from the point of view of reconnaissance. He thought it quite possible the war might be of lengthy duration, and enemy ships might well operate as raiders in Pacific waters. The cable station was also considered to be a "most satisfactory objective for an enemy raider"; early advice of the location of enemy ships, Rosenthal thought, would be invaluable to the Royal Australian Navy and New Zealand Division of the Royal Navy, as well as to the protection of local defence installations and the cable station. The department, however, replied in the negative as it had in 1938. The government's attitude remained unchanged until early April 1942, when Vice Admiral Ghormley was appointed to the South Pacific Command.[6]

Although the war had seemed distant in 1940, the Norfolk Island residents supported Britain with "unquestioned loyalty to the Empire's cause". The Norfolk Island Infantry Detachment, a military unit of volunteers for overseas service, was created under government authority, and by 30 June 1940 the unit had completed 77 days of training. One year later Rosenthal reported that 80 young Islanders, approximately ten per cent of the population, had volunteered for service overseas and they had all been accepted either by the New Zealand forces or the second imperial force.[7]

The Norfolk Island division of the Australian Red Cross continued its activities and raised £377 7s 2d towards the war effort, and donations of oranges and other goods were sent to the New South Wales division of the Australian Red Cross for distribution in hospitals and convalescent homes. The Australian Comforts Fund was formed and regular parcels were sent to Norfolk Island soldiers serving abroad.[8]

Early in 1942 a small Australian detachment of 57 all ranks was sent to Norfolk Island to reinforce the island's detachment and to prevent sabotage of the cable station and its equipment. When the New Zealand Government required assistance from Australia with the defence of New Caledonia, in which reference was made to Norfolk Island, the Commonwealth Government maintained its earlier attitude to the need of an aerodrome on the island. The reply stated that the island was "primarily a naval responsibility and that any aerodrome constructed on it would be more of a liability than an asset". But the new commander of the South Pacific Command, Vice Admiral Ghormley, thought otherwise. He thought that Norfolk Island was in a "unique position" and that it would be of great strategic value as it could act as a kind of "stationary aircraft carrier", serving as a base for anti-submarine patrols, an emergency landing facility for aircraft in distress, and as a staging post for aircraft flying long distances over water between Australia, New Zealand, New Caledonia, and the Solomon Islands.[9]

Ghormley immediately planned for a garrison to defend the island to prevent a possible landing of any raiding parties, and he set about plans for the construction of an aerodrome capable of accommodating the largest aeroplanes. The former Melanesian Mission lands area, a survey of which had been carried out by the Commonwealth staff surveyor R J Rain in 1923, was chosen as the best site available.[10]

In August 1942 an advance party of American and Australian engineers arrived at the island to finally assess the site and to prepare for the arrival of 200 workmen from the Australian Department of Main Roads, who were to carry out the preliminary work. The next month, Ghormley dispatched 4,400 tons of plant and equipment for the construction of two runways. Due to the lack of a harbour, however, the only way to land the heavy machinery was by lightering from ships lying in the open roadstead. This presented a most difficult task for the watermen, but they accomplished the task without loss or accident of any kind.[11]

The site selected included two of the island's main arterial routes, Ferny Lane and Pine Avenue, but to the great sorrow of the Islanders, the latter route required felling a mile-long avenue of 100-year old Norfolk Island pines. The large area of land set aside for the airfield allowed for two runways, one a little over 1800 metres long, with steel matting strip laid for two-thirds of its length over a paved surface of sand and clay, and the other nearly 1700 metres long with a paved surface of crushed metal. Navigational aids were installed including a homing beacon, radio beacon, radio range, high and medium frequency direction-finding, and radar. There was also night-flying equipment in the form of an electric flare-path, searchlight, and a flashing identification beacon. This equipment was essential for the safety of pilots and aircraft,

World War II and Post-War Reconstruction: 1940 to 1965 151

and it was important to the successful prosecution of the war. As the war situation had improved by 1944, the original area of land set aside for the airfield was deemed unnecessary and the size was reduced.[12]

The New Zealand war cabinet also approved the establishment of a garrison force on Norfolk Island, and in October 1942 a force known as N Force, from the 3rd New Zealand Division, consisting of 1,488 all ranks under Lieutenant Colonel J W Barry, Commander of the 36th Battalion, was assembled and dispatched to the island. Barry established headquarters in the house and grounds of Devon, and unit camps were scattered at scenic vantage points around the 37 kilometres of rocky coastline. After defence plans were operational, the New Zealand engineers set up a typical Kiwi procedure – a roading and camp construction plan under Captain W P Hitchcock. They restored a disused sawmill that soon produced 27,542m3 of timber per month; they built a twenty-bed hospital and metalled earth and clay roads around the camps and aerodrome, the maintenance of which the engineers took over on 5 March; and they grew fruit and vegetables for their own use and contributed in other ways to assist island life.

Only six months later, the first group of N Force rejoined the 3rd Division and were replaced by the 2nd Battalion, the Wellington West Coast Regiment, under Lieutenant Colonel A R Cockerell, DSO, who took over the island defences from Barry on 9 April 1943. Three months later the war in the South Pacific had eased and the strength of N Force was reduced. By September, the strategic situation on Norfolk Island was further improved and, in the opinion of the South Pacific Command, a garrison was no longer necessary, except to operate and maintain the airfield. On 8 December 1943, 478 members of the garrison embarked for Auckland. A small rear party remained until 11 February 1944, on which date command passed to the officer commanding the Royal New Zealand Air Force station at the aerodrome, and Norfolk Island became an air force responsibility until 1948.[13]

During the period of the N Force occupation of the island there were some inconveniences felt by residents, but life in general continued almost as normal. The shortage of manpower for agricultural work due to enlistments for war and other special activities were problems, but the Islanders gave dedicated support to the war and made generous financial contributions to various charitable events.

The construction of the aerodrome was completed early in 1943, but the first plane landing was not scheduled. On 25 December 1942 a plan for a New Zealand aircraft to make a parachute drop of Christmas mail and special foods for the men at the garrison failed, but the pilot of one of the aircraft managed to land his plane on the nearly completed landing strip and deliver the Christmas parcels to the eagerly awaiting airmen.[14]

The news of Germany's collapse and its unconditional surrender to the Allies on 8 May 1945 was "joyously received" in Norfolk Island. Over 80 men had served in the navy, army, and air force in all theatres of war but only one had been reported killed in action. There were, however, "many" prisoners of war, both in Germany and Japan, but Rosenthal was confident that these men would soon be repatriated home. With the cessation of hostilities, the residents of the island looked forward to a significantly improved economic future, assisted by the advent of modern transport and communications and, in particular, the aerodrome. The administrator noted in his *Annual Report* that most island families had close relatives serving in the armed forces who were, naturally, very anxious about their welfare, but in reality, there was little to indicate that the territory had been engaged in a war "which represented a life or death struggle for democracy".[15]

Although the Islanders recognised, after the declaration of war, that they too were part of the conflict, the people carried on with their daily lives as they had always done. Their various gatherings and activities were held and the advisory council continued to meet to represent the people of the island and watch over community affairs.

Separation of powers

The concept of the separation of power between government and the judiciary is fundamental to justice in a British democracy. It is hardly surprising that members of the council protested over a long period of time that this basic right was denied them in the courts of Norfolk Island.

At a meeting of the advisory council on 6 May 1940 the president proposed a motion on this issue that had been a source of concern in the community for many years. The president, W McLachlan, proposed that the Judiciary Ordinance 1936 be amended to provide for a visiting stipendiary magistrate instead of a resident chief magistrate, to hear cases in the court in accordance with the council's unanimous resolution of 8 December 1939, and in accordance with its previous representations in 1936 and 1937. Acting on repeated requests from the general public the council reiterated its opinion:

> that the judiciary be entirely divorced from the Administration and that the ends of justice would be better served by the appointment of a visiting Stipendiary Magistrate unconnected with local public affairs and local social obligations and with no previous history of direct participation in highly contentious matters affecting the Administration of the Territory.

Fourteen years before the May meeting, Commissioner Whysall had referred to this unsatisfactory position in hearing cases that came before the court in his 1926 royal commission report. He wrote:

> There is very clear proof in the evidence relating to the administration of justice that the present system is the cause of much dissatisfaction and unrest in the minds of the inhabitants of Norfolk Island.

Whysall found that evidence of the current system had shown that it admitted of "partiality" and that it had been responsible for the "miscarriage of justice in cases dealt with both by the Administrator as Chief Magistrate, and a recently appointed Justice, sitting alone".

The administrator, Colonel Leane, was also "fully appreciative of the difficulties confronting an officer charged with the dual responsibilities of administrator and Chief Magistrate" and his evidence supported the council's views on the present position. But no change in the situation was made.[16]

Further protests and petitions on this matter persisted over the 1930s. The council raised the issue with Sir George Pearce on his visit to the island in 1934. Members of the council complained that the administrator had "excessive and unwarranted powers, both judicial and administrative". Although Pinney was instructed to refer all minor matters to the minister, he was able to secure new ordinances without the people's consent that "vitally affected the peace and welfare of the community".

It was, they argued, "inimical to the interests of peace, order and good government that the administrative and judicial authorities be vested in one man".[17]

A public meeting was held on 20 March 1935 at which the Norfolk Island Association made a considerable number of charges against the administration. A report of the proceedings of the meeting and the recommendations made by the association appeared in prime minister's minutes dated 4 April 1935. One of the numerous charges against the administration referred to the question of the separation of powers. The sixth stated that there was a "serious lack of confidence in the administration of justice; it [was] anomalous that the Administrator should also be Chief Magistrate". A list of recommendations followed the association's statement, the first of which asked that the administrator should be a "gentleman of a temperament compatible with the social conditions of the Island and/or preferably with a sound legal, agricultural and/or commercial ability; he should be appointed solely to administer the affairs of the Island and should not hold the position of Chief Magistrate".[18] Other recommendations concerned a provision for the appointment of a bench of magistrates. It was suggested that four or five reputable residents, in equal numbers of Pitcairners and mainlanders, should act as justices of the peace. The bench:

> could hear and determine any matter within the civil and criminal jurisdiction of the Court except in respect of any sum or matter at issue or respecting property or any civil right above the amount or value of £20 and except upon the investigation of any charge declared indictable or upon the trial of any person charged with an indictable offence against the law of the Territory.

Civil and criminal matters outside the scope of the bench were to be referred by them to a visiting magistrate appointed by the governor-general when necessary, and provision for the right of appeal from the Magistrate's Court to the High Court of Australia should also be made.[19]

Attempts to rectify the untenable state of the current law were made the next year. A Committee of the whole of the advisory council was held on 1 May 1936 to discuss the draft Judiciary Ordinance 1936 and the draft Administration Ordinance 1936. After completing their deliberations the committee reverted to council. The outcome of the meeting proposed that several changes should be made to the Judiciary Ordinance 1936. This Ordinance "to establish a Court for the Territory of Norfolk Island" was subsequently passed on 12 August 1936. Some of the council's recommendations were incorporated in the new Ordinance.

With regard to the Administration Ordinance 1936, the council declared that the draft was not in keeping with the minister's statement of 4 and 5 April 1935, viz:

> I think that the cure for this state of affairs is to divorce the judiciary from the administration. It is always unwise to associate the two positions . . . and the proposal we have in mind is to appoint three or four of the reputable citizens as honorary Justices of the Peace, investing them with jurisdiction to deal with minor offences. The more serious civil and criminal offences could be dealt with by an officer of the Crown Law Department clothed with the powers of a Stipendiary Magistrate, or a magistrate of New South Wales, who could visit Norfolk Island when required . . . I have no doubt that all cases could be disposed of quickly, so that the Stipendiary Magistrate could return to the mainland by the next steamer.

The council did not approve this Ordinance and suggested that it be redrafted "on lines more in keeping with the Minister's proposals to Parliament, and his promises to the people of this Island".[20]

Despite protests, an Ordinance relating to the administration of Norfolk Island (No. 14 of 1936), cited as the Administration Ordinance 1936, was passed on the same day as the previous Ordinance. It repealed the five earlier ordinances that had been in operation from 1913 – but it made no provision for the appointment of a visiting magistrate.

The community requested that this issue should be resolved over subsequent years, but legislation to correct this anomaly was not enacted until the 1980s. In 1985 six magistrates from the Magistrates Court of the Australian Capital Territory were commissioned to appear at the Norfolk Island Court of Petty Sessions. At the same time a number of local residents were appointed as lay magistrates. Currently, the Norfolk Island Court of Petty Sessions is usually presided over by a bench of three lay magistrates appointed by the administrator. In more difficult cases, Australian magistrates from the Australian Capital Territory join the lay magistrates. All magistrates, however, are appointed by the administrator.

1940s and economic development

While acknowledging the extensive hardships felt by the people of the island during the war, M L Treadgold, economic historian, has found that it "profoundly affected the economy of Norfolk Island".

Following the instability of the population statistics over the 1930s, a major outflow of the civilian population occurred during the war years as young men left to join the forces and others left to be near their enlisted relatives on the mainland. In consequence there were severe labour shortages; external communication links were changed and foreign trade was disrupted and reduced to the level of the worst years of the 1930s depression. Local activities were, of necessity, restructured, but this was only short-lived; the pre-war pattern of development, on the other hand, was never fully restored. It was replaced by a "new pattern of development which was itself in large part a legacy of the war".[21]

Aside from the significant loss of the nine young soldiers who died in battle and those who were captured or injured, there were two other long-term costs resulting from the war: neglect and deterioration of the agricultural and pastoral industries and a loss of a good deal of the timber reserves.[22]

The running down of their agricultural and pastoral industries due to lack of labour and wear and tear on the physical capital invested in these industries led to a serious curtailment of production and decline in export income. Even after the rural workforce returned to the island, production capacity in the farming sector lagged behind pre-war levels for a number of years. The effect of wartime neglect was obvious in the state of the land. It had become overgrown with noxious weeds that spread out of control and plants such as lantana, tobacco bush, and Cape tulip were firmly established. Insects, pests, and plant diseases ran rampant. The vine leaf hopper (*Scolypopa australis*) bred freely in the lantana and tobacco bush and then attacked the passionfruit vines; other bacterial diseases spread through the various island crops. The old orange trees, an earlier source of export income, had not been replanted and the trees were no longer productive. And the stock of cattle, slaughtered to provide beef for the New Zealand garrison and local population, was significantly depleted and inadequate for the needs of the Islanders.[23]

The timber reserves were another charge on the economy, as they were further depleted by wartime demands. From early days the settlers had allowed their cattle to roam unrestricted over the island, thus causing damage to the natural regeneration of the native pine and other trees. When fruit exports boomed in the 1920s, timber for packing cases was required. This, together with the ongoing need for timber for building and fencing, had a significant impact on timber supplies. C E Lane Poole, a Commonwealth forestry expert, had proposed a forestry policy for the island after his visit in 1925, but it was only partially implemented, and therefore had only limited effect. The military occupation in the 1940s also added to the increasing demand for timber, mainly for construction purposes. As a consequence, the remaining forests were "almost entirely denuded of accessible hardwood" and "heavy inroads were made on the Norfolk Island pine". A report years later stated that "probably half the existing timber on the Island [had] either been utilised, destroyed or [had] died".[24]

Despite the toll on island resources at this time, there were two long-term benefits that were a direct result of the war, and they had a major effect on the post-war economy. The main benefit was the construction of the airfield. This has been identified as "the single most important event in the Island's twentieth century economic history"; its importance to the residents and the economy today is as relevant as it was in 1942.[25]

The advent of an air service for passengers made travel to Norfolk Island easy and enabled the emergence of a thriving tourism industry; it also provided an improved form of transport for the island's export trade. For the large number of people who had served officially on the island during the war and enjoyed the beauty of the island, the new air service made a visit to the island for leisure purposes both possible and desirable. The tourism industry was significantly assisted by this development as the potential for the island as a tourist destination became apparent in the outside world.

In addition to this, Norfolk Island's role in the war – its strategic value in the Pacific and the people's contribution to the armed services and war effort – meant that awareness and knowledge of the island had spread to Australia and New Zealand in both private and government spheres. The effect of this was that post-war growth in tourism (with its associated infrastructure) in the private sector and a concern for the economic welfare of the community in government arose. The Commonwealth, as a result, gave a good deal of technical and financial assistance: experts and consultants were sent to the island to advise on agriculture, forestry, and other matters. By the end of the 1950s direct budgetary aid in the form of Commonwealth grants was "in total nominal terms about eight times as high as it had been immediately prior to the war". World War II, Treadgold claimed, laid the foundations for a "pattern of economic activity" that differed markedly from the Island's pre-war experience".[26]

International and local news

From the early signs of war, island residents were kept well informed about its development, locally and overseas. News from Europe reached Norfolk Island via the cable and wireless station at Anson Bay. Before 3 September 1939 the *Norfolk Island Weekly*, owned and published by A S Gazzard, featured reports from overseas. A report relayed from the London *Daily Telegraph*, headed "Increase in German naval strength", was published in the *Weekly* on 8 January 1939, and it was followed by successive items about Germany's plans and the strength of the British forces. An article dated 13 January 1939, headed

"Recruiting March in Sydney", notified the public about a military parade of around 3,000 men who were to march in the streets of Sydney on 10 February.

Through the war years Gazzard's newspaper featured extensive coverage in regular reports of "The War Day by Day". In addition to the establishment of the earlier Norfolk Island Infantry Detachment, the *Weekly* reported the formation of a Norfolk Island Volunteer Reserve in 1941 as the war situation deteriorated. A meeting of the Committee of Returned Soldiers was later held on 8 February to discuss the details of the new organisation. The Reserve was to select its own officers and NCOs and was to place the organisation at the disposal of the Officer in Charge of the Infantry Detachment. The minutes of the meeting, signed on behalf of the committee by F R M Crozier, stated: "We should be ready for every contingency".[27]

The meeting ruled that members of the Reserve were to include several groups. The first group comprised over-age soldiers and men working in reserved occupations. In the second, those with cars were to form a Volunteer Motor Transport Corps to assist in emergency troop transport, supplies, and in any other possible way. A third group was made up of nurses, persons with first-aid certificates, and helpers, who were to form the staff for an auxiliary hospital and perform duties at first-aid posts. Finally, the meeting agreed to appoint two men to "keep an eye" on stocks of essential foodstuffs and approach the administrator if supplies were running short. The meeting chose three residents to receive members and organise the groups for duty: F J Tattle headed the Fighting Reserve; A J McGrath, the Motor Transport, and Colonel Baird took charge of the auxiliary hospital.

The densely written *Norfolk Island Weekly*, a wax sheet production printed by duplicator, contained letters, local news and events as well as reports of the war. The newspaper ceased publication soon after the death of the editor on 18 October 1943; from that time there was no local newspaper until the administration published the *Norfolk News* in 1958.

The first edition of the *Norfolk Island Weekly* was issued on 22 January 1937, eight years before Gazzard's death. Extant issues range from 1937–1943 but the folio is incomplete. Over the life of the *Weekly* various matters of public interest were printed, two of which raised significant objections from the Islanders: the first was connected with the publication of the advisory council minutes, and the second concerned the discontinuance of the special page for *Government Gazette* notices that had been included in the *Weekly*.

The controversy over publication of the council minutes arose later in 1939. Council meetings were open to the public, thus from 1932 successive local newspapers published items of interest reported from the proceedings of council meetings. A great deal of information was disseminated in that way.

In 1935 the *Norfolk Island Times* (published from 1933 to 1935) printed items of interest from the meetings, but the newspaper was discontinued that same year, and no newspaper immediately followed. The Islanders, therefore, requested that the advisory council minutes be posted at the Tree of Knowledge on the corner of Burnt Pine and Harpers roads and at Middlegate within three days after each council meeting, signed provisionally by the president, for the information of the people; and, in addition, an anonymous resident had offered to supply glass-fronted cases for the display of the notices.

This method of informing the public probably took place and survived up to the commencement of the new *Norfolk Island Weekly* in which the advisory council minutes were published.²⁸

This arrangement worked satisfactorily until November 1939, when the administrator cabled the minister advising him that the wording of the advisory council resolution on the estimates had been "insulting and objectionable". He considered it "most undesirable" that the minutes be posted on the noticeboard or published in the *Norfolk Island Weekly*. He proposed prohibition of publication until the minutes were submitted for the minister's approval.

The offending minutes, accompanied by a memorandum from the administrator dated 12 December 1939, were sent to the minister. Rosenthal informed him that the advisory council sat with "open doors" and proceedings were open to the public. In his opinion, minutes of the "type under review should not be published in the local newspaper and thus be available for sending out of the Island" to, perhaps, be used by the mainland press to criticise the administration. Rosenthal added that it was not mandatory to publish the minutes, as there was no provision for this in the Advisory Council Ordinance. He explained that as a result of one "objectionable" minute, the government medical officer had taken action for damages against the mover of the resolution. Rosenthal, as a result, recommended that owing to the "objectionable, inaccurate and in some cases defamatory statements" made in the newspaper, no council minutes should be published in the *Norfolk Island Weekly* or posted at the courthouse, Kingston, until they had been reviewed by the minister. He suggested publication of the minutes be prohibited unless the council was prepared "to rescind all resolutions and resubmit them in suitable and courteous language".

The attorney-general's advice was sought, and his reply dated 4 January 1940 stated from a "legal standpoint the only objections that could be raised to the publication of the minutes by the Administrator would be that they might contain libellous matter and that publication would thus make the Administrator liable for an action for libel at the instance of any person in respect of whom defamatory statements were in the minutes". The department advised that:

> while the proceedings of the Council may be privileged it did not follow that reports of those proceedings would be likewise privileged and if the Administrator had any doubt as to the propriety of anything said in a meeting of the council and included in the minutes it would be advisable for him not to publish or have any hand in the publication of the minutes of such meeting.

The attorney-general further advised that from a political point of view, it appeared to be preferable that the administrator inform the council that he would not publish or have any hand in the publication of the council minutes in future; the reason to be given being that "certain resolutions" relating to the 1939–1940 estimates "were couched in terms which might be held to be libellous". This advice was given to Rosenthal for "his information only". The minister gave no decision and the matter was left to the administrator. As he was under no official obligation to publish the minutes, Rosenthal chose not to do so.[29]

This matter surfaced again on three occasions during 1942.

Referring to its democratic right, the council proposed that the minutes be published "for the benefit and general interest of the public". On 14 October 1942 Rosenthal wrote to the Department of External Affairs that the:

> resolution that the minutes of the Advisory Council should be published has been previously answered on two other occasions. No good purpose will be served to publishing these minutes, which are of no interest to others than Members of the Council and the Publisher of the *Norfolk Island Weekly*. Not the slightest interest is taken by the public either in the Council or its doings.[30]

A history of developments in this dispute was prepared for the prime minister the next year, and on 4 January 1943 the administrator received a cablegram signed: "PRIMISTER". The cable stated that the department was "aware" of the circumstances under which publication of the minutes was prohibited, but it was suggested that "unless there are likely to be harmful results the time [had] arrived to permit the publication of such minutes" and it was felt that the community's lack of interest in the "doings" of the council might, thus, be revived.

Overlapping the dispute regarding the minutes, the administrator, perhaps with mixed feelings and irritation with certain members of the council and concerned for the security of the island in wartime, advised the editor of the *Norfolk Island Weekly* that the arrangements to publish the *Government Gazette* notices on a special page in the *Norfolk Island Weekly* would be discontinued after 31 December 1942. The notices, instead, were to be posted on the noticeboards. Rosenthal's memorandum to the minister stated that Gazzard made "many departures from the rules of censorship and other doubtful activities" and that this was the reason for the cancellation.

The editor, however, enlisted the support of the advisory council. In his letter of 18 January 1943 to the council, Gazzard claimed that he had not been given a reason for the discontinuance of the *Gazette* page and that information was no longer easily accessible to the general public. The council supported Gazzard and pursued the complaint with the government. The matter was then referred to the Prime Minister's Department. The matter, however, was marked "outstanding" on 19 February 1943, and it was noted that "further action" was being taken. There is no record of a subsequent meeting or decision on this issue, but it appeared that the issue was allowed to drop.[31]

Gazzard's particular interest in the continuation of publication of the minutes and the *Government Gazette* page in the newspaper was no doubt related to the financial remuneration he received from the administration. Rosenthal had recently increased the contract price to the paper from £1 per week to £1 5s as a result of a rise in the cost of paper; this, Gazzard acknowledged, greatly assisted in keeping the *Weekly* in circulation.[32]

At the 9 July meeting six months later, the council passed a recommendation that the administrator reinstate the *Gazette* page in the *Norfolk Island Weekly*, as due to old age or lack of transport "very few people" were able to read the noticeboards, and they were anxious that they may incur a penalty for failure to register their vote at elections.

It seems that the crisis over the minutes and the *Gazette*

page had repercussions on 17 September 1943 when Gazzard proposed that:

> as the defamation laws of the States of the Commonwealth protect newspapers which publish fair and accurate reports of the proceedings at Parliament, similar laws be introduced on Norfolk Island, giving protections to newspapers which publish fair and accurate reports of the proceedings of the Advisory Council.

Gazzard wanted the same protection to apply on the island by an amendment to the Printers and Newspapers Ordinance 1935–1936 but this was "not recommended" by the administrator.

In forwarding copies of the October–November council minutes to Canberra, Rosenthal notified the minister of an anomaly that had existed in council for the past three years. Due to the "total lack of interest" shown by the community in advisory council affairs there had been no nominations for election at council beyond those of retiring members each year. Consequently, "no election" was necessary as retiring members were automatically returned. Rosenthal deplored this situation as being detrimental to community life. Gazzard had been "responsible" for the majority of the resolutions passed in council, and he was "undoubtedly" using his position as a councillor in the interest of his newspaper and against the administration.[33]

The question of the minutes, the *Gazette* page, and the protection of newspapers was ultimately resolved by Gazzard's death on 18 October 1943: his newspaper subsequently closed. From that time there was no local newspaper until the administration published the *Norfolk News* in 1958. The Printers and Newspapers Ordinance 1935–1936 together with a number of other ordinances, were later repealed by the Ordinance Revision Ordinance 1964 as they were by that time redundant.[34]

Postal services and banking

Norfolk Island established its own postal administration with full facilities in June 1947, and at the same time the first of a long line of colourful island stamps was issued. Prior to this, letters from Norfolk had been stamped with issues from Tasmania, New South Wales, and the Commonwealth of Australia. The stamps of Tasmania used initially in Norfolk from 1834 until April 1856 dated from the island's second penal settlement, when it was annexed to Tasmania. This stamp was identified by a "72" numeral cancellation.

Little is known of postal arrangements between 1856 and 1897, when the third settlement was transferred to the Governor of Norfolk Island. The deputy administrator of Norfolk Island, who was based at the Department of Lands in Sydney, conducted the affairs of the island in conjunction with the resident administrator, the governor, and New South Wales government until 1913. When the passage of the *Norfolk Island Act 1913* transferred the island to become a territory of the Commonwealth, the Norfolk Island administration conducted postal services as part of the Commonwealth postal system, and Australian stamps were used. On 10 June 1947 the island produced its own first issue of stamps. Depicting the distinctive

Norfolk Island pine, these stamps were in great demand for sale overseas.[35]

In the gap of 42 years between 1856 and 1897 of the third settlement, it is uncertain what provision was made for outgoing mail. There was, apparently, some arrangement made as a dispatch for Lord Loftus to the Colonial Office dated 9 March 1885, stating that he had:

> arranged with the Postmaster General [Sydney] that stamps shall be forwarded to the Postmaster at Norfolk Island, for which he will be responsible to this Post Office and that the letters etc. shall, as heretofore be forwarded to the Sydney Post Office".

Prior to any official method of forwarding mail, outgoing letters probably found their way to Australia and elsewhere by private arrangement on board visiting vessels willing to make the deliveries.[36]

The *Norfolk Island Act 1913* commenced on 1 July 1914. In the 1916 *Annual Report* the administrator, M V Murphy, announced that the Post Office was open for the transaction of business on and after the arrival of vessels from Sydney, Auckland, or the New Hebrides. There were usually two outward and two inward mails per month, with some two to four additional casual mails during the year. There was, in addition, a money order office and branch of the Commonwealth Savings Bank of Australia opened on 1 July 1915 and it had proved to be a "great public convenience". It was hoped that the "limited operations" of the savings bank would be extended to meet the requirements of employers and enable them to have money transmitted from the Commonwealth Bank in Sydney, by telegraph, to the branch in Norfolk Island. The money order and savings bank was conducted through an agency at the Post Office.[37]

Before the establishment of the Commonwealth Savings Bank agency, it appears that there was an earlier system for banking that continued for 40 years alongside the administration's agency. Initially, after the arrival of the Pitcairners, a barter system operated on the island, even though there was "a little money in circulation". In 1881 the Norfolk Island Penny Savings Bank was established. Franklin Bates was its manager in 1885 with W Quintal as accountant. The bank was situated on Pine Avenue and the managing trustee was F W Pearson. The government auditor carried out the annual audit, and copies of the balance sheet were posted on the public noticeboards. The Norfolk Island Penny Savings Bank Ordinance 1935 latterly covered the bank's activities.[38]

In 1949 it was hoped that a trading bank would soon be opened at Norfolk Island when financial operations increased to the necessary level. This, however, did not happen until 1956, when a new branch of the Commonwealth Savings Bank of Australia opened in addition to the local agency connected to the Post Office. This new branch represented the first trading bank – the Commonwealth Trading Bank of Australia – that operated as an agency within the savings bank.[39]

Norfolk Island's public hospitals

As Atlee Hunt pointed out in his report of 1913, there was only one hospital on Norfolk Island – situated on the Mission Estate

– but it was not available to the general public. He recommended that as soon as funds permitted, a small cottage should be built and properly equipped for this purpose, and a trained nurse placed in charge.[40]

Hunt's suggestion did not become reality until the 1920s, when the administrator, Major General V C M Sellheim, opened the Cottage Hospital on 10 November 1927. It was a government building, convict-built, and located at 6 Quality Row. The government medical officer, Dr L S Duke, lived nearby and was in charge of the hospital. The vacant building was newly converted from a residential dwelling to one suitable for a hospital, and it contained two wards, each containing two beds, and a verandah ward of one bed. Quarters were provided for one trained nurse and two probationers. The well-equipped theatre and sterilising room were adjacent, and the kitchen/dining room and bathroom completed the hospital complex. Miss Gordina Nobbs, trained nurse, was appointed Matron. She became Mrs Gordina Beveridge some months later, but she maintained a long and valuable association with the hospital until her late years.

Control of the hospital was vested in a board of five – four elected annually by vote at a public meeting and one, the government medical officer, an ex-officio member. C C R Nobbs was president and E Stephenson, honorary secretary and treasurer. Finance for the new institution was arranged by local collections, hospital fees, and subscriptions from the general public; and the Ladies' Auxiliary Committee raised funds through organised entertainments. The administration contributed other financial assistance by a pound for pound subsidy based on expenditure.[41]

World War II and Post-War Reconstruction: 1940 to 1965 173

Two years after Dr Duke established the Cottage Hospital, the Secretary of the Melanesian Mission Trust Board, Auckland, wrote to the minister for home and territories on 27 February 1929, enclosing a plan for a proposed subdivision of the mission land they had vacated in 1920. If the scheme was approved the board planned "to lease for the purpose of a public hospital Lot 9 with the Bishop's house standing thereon" as well as leases for other purposes. The board had not then decided upon the terms for which each lease would be granted, but it was stated that the board "would be glad to receive any guidance [on] this matter which the [minister might] see fit to offer".

About the same time members of the Norfolk Island Hospital Board approached the prime minister. This letter of 1 May 1929 explained the present situation with regard to the inadequate hospital accommodation. The board recalled that almost two years before a small four-bed hospital had been established in a vacant government building; but the community had outgrown this arrangement and the "climatic conditions" at Kingston were not "conducive to the well-being of patients as those obtaining at higher altitudes on the Island". The board had felt "compelled" to approach the Melanesian Mission Trust Board with a view to obtaining the bishop's house as a hospital building. The five members of the hospital board signed the letter and urged the prime minister to take action "as soon as possible".

The *Annual Report* for 1930 recorded that:

> [following] negotiations between the Norfolk Island Hospital Board and the Melanesian Mission Trust Board the lease was obtained of the building known as "Bishop's House", situated

on the Mission property, together with 9 acres of land, at a weekly rental of £2. 10. 0. The removal from Kingston to the new Mission site was effected by 8 June 1930.[42]

The next year a prime minister's minute of 9 December 1931 advised that the department had received an enquiry from the Norfolk Island Hospital Board as to whether the Commonwealth Government would be willing to insert a clause in the document for the proposed lease (9 acres, two roads) on which the bishop's house stood, which would give the island hospital board an option to purchase the land. The minister had already consented to the lease of the block to the hospital board, but members then expressed the opinion that the public would "more readily" support the hospital if it were known that there was a possibility of eventually acquiring the property. As the administrator supported this request, the minister consented to its inclusion in the document of lease.[43]

By 1936 the layout of the hospital at the bishop's house had proved unsatisfactory. Plans were prepared for a new hospital to be built at Middlegate on a roughly 3-hectare site that had been reserved for hospital purposes since April 1932. Two years after Administrator Rosenthal reported, the financial position of the hospital was "not yet satisfactory due to a large sum of money still outstanding against patients for hospital treatment". This sum, on the other hand, was being gradually reduced. He noted that the present building was "not well suited for the purpose while the rent [was] relatively high", but that the fund for the new building had reached £159 10s 8d. It was hoped that work on the first section of the new hospital would soon commence.[44]

While the hospital fund gradually increased over the next few years, the onset of war and shortages of labour and building materials delayed the start of the project. In 1945 the *Annual Report* stated that the "present hospital buildings [were] in urgent need of many improvements and repairs". The board agreed that expenditure on those buildings would not be justified, pending a decision as to whether or not the Royal New Zealand Air Force station hospital could be taken over by the board and administered as a civil hospital. Negotiations with regard to the future of the hospital proceeded for the next two years. It was decided to erect a new, modern hospital at the central site occupied by the temporary structure used as the Royal New Zealand Air Force hospital, and the board's hopes were realised the next year when work commenced.[45]

Construction of the new building proceeded, but work was seriously delayed due to the inability to obtain the necessary building supplies from Australia. The administrator reported that the new building was designed to provide modern facilities, and it was to be big enough to cope with a large number of patients in an emergency. It would, however, increase maintenance and staff costs, but in view of the development of the island as a tourist resort and the substantial increase in air passengers carried, it was felt that the territory should be prepared to meet any substantial emergency hospitalisation problems.[46]

Despite unavoidable delay, building commenced, and the minister for territories, the Honourable Paul Hasluck, opened the hospital on 21 March 1952. The following year the Norfolk Island Public Hospital Ordinance 1953, which provided for the control and management of the new hospital, came into force on 7 April 1953. In accordance with section 7 of the Ordinance, five persons were appointed to be members of the Norfolk Island Public Hospital Board. They were: Frankyn C Christian, Tom C Lee, Mrs Gordina Beveridge, Mrs Kathleen Walsh, and William McLachlan.

Prior to the promulgation of the Hospital Ordinance, however, the previous hospital board had not been properly constituted, hence it had no legal constitution, and management and control of the hospital was difficult and unsatisfactory. To remedy this unsatisfactory legal situation, Administrator H B Norman released the members of the board in order to restructure the board as a legal entity. The advisory council, on the other hand, objected, believing Norman's actions to "release" board members was just another negation of the council's rights. In his reply of 7 May 1953 to the council, Norman explained that the previous board had been "unconstitutional", and "in the event of any legal action against it, the individual members and not the Board would be required to defend the suit". As the board had not been a statutory body with a body corporate, Norman believed that he had "no right" to ask the board members to continue in such a vulnerable position. Action, therefore, was immediately taken to procure the relevant ordinance, on receipt of which it was posted at the courthouse and a new board was appointed.[47]

As the population grew and circumstances demanded, the hospital complex was extended incorporating other necessary facilities, and the separate buildings were connected by covered walkways.[48]

1950s and 1960s – customs and councils

In the immediate post-war years, during which postal and banking services were extended and a legally constituted public hospital established, relations between the administration and the advisory council were reasonably untroubled; but this quiescent period ended on 30 November 1954 when a new customs ordinance was posted at the courthouse. The people's reaction to this Ordinance gave rise to a series of potent clashes between the council on the one hand, and government authorities on the other, and they were not resolved until 1964.

At the first advisory council meeting after the proclamation, held on 8 December 1954, the members' angry response to the Ordinance dominated the proceedings. Councillor G G F Quintal proposed that as the matter was "one of urgency"; it should be dealt with immediately and "take priority over all other business". Correspondence received from a number of individuals was tabled; W N Selby Newbald's letter of 2 December referred to the 'iniquitous Ordinance" and castigated the government on its "undemocratic approach" and "lack of consideration for the people and the future of [the] Island". Commenting on the "already too high" taxes on "living essentials", he slated the government's dictatorial approach "to solve the troubles of a wasteful and spendthrift Administration". He pushed for a vote of no confidence and censure in the administrator and an *immediate repeal* by cable or the council "should resign en bloc". Other negative criticisms followed and after lengthy discussions, Councillor A B Commins proposed:

That this Council asks the Administrator to cable the Minister for Territories, requesting him to favourably consider the immediate repeal of the Customs Ordinance 1934 which was made without first being submitted to the Advisory Council.

A petition signed by 375 residents was addressed to Her Majesty the Queen, Buckingham Palace, on 26 January 1955. It stated that the Customs Ordinance 1954 was "contrary to the fundamental principle of British Government that there shall be no taxation without representation" and it beseeched the Queen to restore to the people the "democratic right of control over [their] domestic affairs". The accompanying letter from R H H Nobbs, chairman and president of the advisory council, explained that the petition was the outcome of the people's protest at a public meeting against a law that had been imposed without the prior knowledge or consent of the council.

Unknown to the Islanders, the council received a great deal of support from Minister for Territories Paul Hasluck. A few months earlier, he had challenged the treasurer, Sir Arthur Fadden, on the sum of the annual grant to be given to Norfolk Island finances. The treasurer had proposed that funds for the islands' expenses, "local services, facilities and assistance should be limited to the revenue it [was] practicable to raise on the Island in any given year and that Commonwealth aid should be limited to expenditure associated with the establishment of the Administrator". Fadden proposed that the grant be £15,000 rather than the £42,000 that had been sought on the basis of the draft estimates.

Hasluck "disagreed entirely" with this proposition. While he agreed that services provided for the residents should not be in excess of those provided in comparable centres of population on the Australian mainland, he stated that the Islanders had already taken steps to raise the level of local revenue, in that import duties had been "completely revised" and should contribute an extra £3,000 per year. The community was, he said, a "comparatively poor one", and there should be "fairly strict limits" placed on any additional burdens imposed.[49] Since a revision of fees and import duties had already been made, it is not surprising the people strongly objected to the new Ordinance.

This event ignited the passions of a number of outspoken residents who united to form the Norfolk Island Citizens' Progress Association. A letter, dated 2 August 1955, from the association to the advisory council submitted a "unanimous" wish that the council write "in the strongest terms" to the minister for territories requesting him to arrange for a parliamentary delegation to visit the island because, they believed, Hasluck had dealt with their request for a "New Constitution" in "an arbitrary way", and they wanted an all-party delegation to investigate their grievances. The "New Constitution" was to give the people "ultimate local control" of island affairs and would be "run on a democratic basis".[50]

A copy of the association's letter reached the administrator, H B Norman, who had not received official notification of the formation of the association. In a memorandum dated 15 September 1955, Norman advised the Department of Territories of the information he had obtained: "from what could be gathered", he said, "it was started by W N S Newbald, H S Newberry, F J Needham, T Bailey, W Simmonds, J Westwood etc and consisted of only about twenty members".

The membership was two shillings, Mr N Summerscale, chairman of the association for the meeting that led to the August letter, had been to see the administrator: "He was very concerned because he did not wish it thought that the contents were his views, as he had joined the Association and been elected Chairman for that particular meeting and thought he was obliged to sign the letter". He went on to say that "he did not like the atmosphere and the implied necessity to sign". Norman noted in the memorandum that there was an "element not willing to permit matters to return to a peaceful footing".

By 9 January 1956 the administrator had apparently received a copy of the association's constitution from the chairman, W N Selby Newbald, who expressed the association's desire to work in "close cooperation" with the administration; and he requested that the association be informed of the government's long-term policy for the welfare of Norfolk Island. Norman's letter to the association set out a draft policy. The main prospects, he said, appeared to be in forestry, agriculture, and the tourism trade; some of his aims covered a forest working plan and expansion of bean seed production, as well as an improved air service and tourism trade, and the encouragement of industry for the island.

Selby Newbald wrote to the minister with the complaint that Norman's policy was only that of a "bird of passage" and it had been the community's "sad experience" that successive administrators differed "entirely" with preceding government policies. This "lack of continuity" in policy was "detrimental" to the economy and precluded any progress.

The minister prepared a paper about 6 April 1956 for members of parliament, setting out historical details of the argument over the Customs Ordinance and the subsequent petitions. The paper revealed that the governor-general's official secretary had been instructed to reply to the council in regard to the petitions. It was stated that the governor-general, as the Queen's representative in Australia, dealt with Australian petitions addressed to Her Majesty. The paper set out the constitutional position on this matter and noted that the citizens of Norfolk Island could, within 30 days after receipt of an ordinance, make representations to the government which would be taken into account when considering whether an ordinance should be repealed or amended; and it was understood that such action had been taken by the council. The Commonwealth Government would consider other matters contained in the petition in the light of the Norfolk Island Act. In these circumstances, the paper stated, the governor-general had "not been pleased to grant the petition" and the council was informed accordingly.

A later section in the paper explained why the government had introduced the new legislation without first advising the council. The Customs Ordinance 1954 was treated as "urgent" because it contained a Customs Schedule. Normal Commonwealth practice was to introduce changes in Custom Schedules in such a way as would avoid the possibility that any individual may gain advantage or be able to manipulate his trading as a result of prior knowledge of the details of the Schedule. On the mainland, details of the Schedule could be kept secret by dating legislation to take effect from the day of publication of the budget proposals. But on the island, the retrospective effect of ordinances was precluded by the Act. The safeguard for the council was that it could make representations for amendments. Hasluck's paper also included a table of comparative custom duties. The figures in the table made it clear that duties paid by the Islanders were considerably lower than those paid by mainlanders; for example, Norfolk Island paid a duty of 2s 6d per gallon for ale or beer, whereas Australians paid 7s 2d per gallon; similarly, Norfolk Island leaf tobacco incurred a duty of 2s per pound whereas the duty in Australia was 14s 5d.

In his reply to Selby Newbald on 5 June 1956, the minister stated:

> in broad terms, the policies adopted by the government for the administration of Norfolk Island, in common with other Territories of the Commonwealth, have as their main objective the development and proper utilisation of the natural resources and the encouragement of industry and trade.

Improvements in living conditions, health, education, and a number of other services were listed in the government's policies.

The upheaval over the Customs Ordinance was relatively short. At the advisory council meeting of 25 March 1955 the administrator tabled a letter from the minister in which he advised the council that he had "carefully considered" the council's requests. Hasluck was not prepared to accede to the council's request to repeal the Ordinance, but he was prepared to amend the Ordinance along the lines of his attached draft, and he indicated his willingness to negotiate further. At the meeting on the same day, two draft amendments were put forward, the second of which was carried. The amended legislation, Customs Ordinance 1955, was posted at the courthouse on 9 April 1955; four successive amendments were proclaimed in the period leading to Customs Ordinance 1963, notified on 1 July. Hasluck's general concern for the well-being of the Islanders assisted in the speedy resolution of this dispute.[51]

As the Islanders recovered their equilibrium and returned to a usual way of life after the traumas of war, long-held attitudes of yearning for independence and self-government gradually resurfaced. In the early 1950s the people's voice grew more insistent than it had been since the war. The Islanders wanted more control in the management and decision-making of community affairs and a voice in the allocation of Island revenue.

A resolution passed at the advisory council meeting of 6 May 1953 declared: "this Council urges that immediate steps be taken to initiate the progressive vesting of executive powers in it or in an elected body that might replace it as foreshadowed by the Minister on his recent visit to the Island". The minister was Paul Hasluck and his statement opened the way for ongoing discussion. The question arose again on 8 July. The council regretted that it had had "such a limited say in the method of spending any of the revenue raised", and it "had not had an opportunity to discuss the estimates of revenue and expenditure".

The main focus of council meetings over the next year was directed towards the unpopular customs legislation, but it was apparent that the wish for power and active input into the administration of local affairs underlay the negotiations over customs. Selby Newbald, who was not a member of council, had challenged council to resign as a body in his December letter. In addition to his criticism of the administration and its handling of the Customs Ordinance 1954, he pressed council for a "compulsory referendum" of residents to be held "to settle for some years ahead the vital interest of those interested in the future prosperity" of the island. He concluded his letter by offering himself "to be co-opted to air the views of those (far too many) who considered the Administration had ignored the essential needs of the people". Newbald's statement signalled trouble, and it culminated in the proclamation of the *Norfolk Island Act 1957* and the subsequent negotiations over the new Norfolk Island Council.

Selby Newbald and the Norfolk Island Progress Association (also known as the Norfolk Island Citizens' Progress Association) initiated a great many of the issues in which it urged the advisory council to act against the authorities. Newbald was a frequent correspondent to council as was the Progress Association. One example of the many intercessions by members of the Progress Association was in relation to Hasluck's answer to a question asked in the House of Representatives. As Hasluck responded in a way that Newbald thought gave members a false impression of conditions on the island, namely that the people's grievances had "diminished", Newbald's letter was tabled at the council meeting on 4 May 1955 and he asked council to consider certain points on which he elaborated. Newbald forcefully called upon the council to pursue the Islanders' petition with the governor-general for "democratic control over their own affairs" and approach the minister stating that the "vast majority" of residents were "not satisfied with taxation without representation"; and he pushed for the minister to arrange for an all-party parliamentary delegation to visit and investigate the true position.[52]

The association aggressively promoted the people's case for reform outside Norfolk Island. The chairman of the Progress Association, F J Needham, approached the South Pacific Commission in a letter dated 15 June 1955. He set out what the association saw as "the main issue" in the current proceedings; this was that the people should have a "democratic constitution representative of the people, controlling expenditure and taxation of at least the monies provided by the people of the Island – perhaps £24,000 per annum". This letter also sought a visit from an "extra-national" body to investigate the Norfolk Island situation.[53]

News of events on Norfolk Island was circulated around the Pacific and as far as the United States of America. The *Christian Science Monitor* of Boston, USA, published an article, "Mutiny Descendants Stir", referring to the "dictatorship" of administrators on Norfolk Island, and the "tyranny" of "taxation without representation". The records are studded with requests for "ultimate local control", a visit by a parliamentary delegation, and a new constitution, as well as other issues, all of which featured on the agenda of Norfolk Island's politics in the lead-up to the *Norfolk Island Act 1957*.[54]

The ward system had been disliked since it was introduced in 1935. When the Progress Association wrote to council on 14 May 1955 proposing that the ward system of voting should be abolished and replaced with an alternative system, the council agreed. A resolution to that effect was passed and the matter was to be brought to the attention of the minister for territories.[55]

In reply to this resolution, the administrator notified the council on 6 December 1955 that the minister wished to know "in what way did Council consider the present system to be defective", and he required details of the system that the council wished to introduce.

The minister received a confirmed resolution on 8 March 1956 setting out the council's reason why it desired to abolish the present system, but it did not state details of a system of election it desired to introduce in its place. That is, unless it meant that all four councillors for election each year should be elected under a similar system of voting to that at present used. The council was asked to clarify the matter.

In reply, the council resolved "that this Council recommends that the present system of voting for Council elections be continued, that is, the four candidates with the greatest number of votes be elected".[56]

The minister noted that the latter part of this resolution conflicted with the earlier part, and the administrator was asked to clarify the matter. Norman's reply on 17 January 1957 advised that he understood:

> that the Advisory Council desired to eliminate the ward system of nomination and institute election from a general nomination. Voting would then be for the same members all over the Territory and those elected would be the four receiving the highest number of votes in any year.

Following clarification of the details, the administrator was asked to inform the advisory council "that the Minister [was] prepared to approve of action being taken to amend the legislation" as finally proposed. The first election was to be held on the first Wednesday in July 1957.[57]

The Progress Association wrote to council again on 12 March 1957. The letter observed that "no action" had been taken since the minister's suggestion in November the year before, and the association pointed out that it was "incumbent" upon the council to implement the change as it stood, and it suggested that the minister's proposal be accepted in time for the forthcoming election. At the same meeting, the administrator referred to council's resolution of 2 January 1957 regarding the election of members to the advisory council, and he tendered the minister's view that "the initiative for any changes in the existing system [lay] with the Council and that the Council's views on this matter should prevail". The minister assumed that the council would incorporate the 2 January decision in the "overall resolution specifying the actual changes which the council wished to have made" and notification of the above resolution was sought.[58]

Before the question of voting could finally be settled, however, the Commonwealth Government, in an effort to meet the community's demands for greater power in Norfolk Island affairs than it had before, passed the *Norfolk Island Act 1957*, assented to on 30 May 1957. This Act provided for a Norfolk Island Council to replace the advisory council, changes in the judicial system, and other legal changes. But the Norfolk Island Council could not be constituted until the 1957 Act had been proclaimed; all subordinate legislation, therefore, was delayed until the advisory council accepted the Act.

The system of voting, however, was subsequently concluded at a meeting of the advisory council on 5 March 1958. To determine the will of the people on this matter, the council held a referendum in July 1957 that asked whether the community favoured the retention of the existing system or one that would abolish the wards and introduce voting on an island-wide basis. Overwhelmingly, the people rejected the old system in favour of the latter method of election.[59]

The years between the governor-general's assent to the *Norfolk Island Act 1957*, which repealed the *Norfolk Island Act 1913*, and the Islanders' acceptance of the new Norfolk Island Council Ordinance 1960 (notified 14 April), was a period when dialogue was complicated and compromise difficult to reach.

The Norfolk Island Council as provided by the Ordinance was a kind of local government body to be established under the 1957 Act. It was to have powers and functions conferred upon it by the Act or by ordinance made in accordance with Part III of the Act. Ordinances dealt with a provision for incorporation of the council, and for council to exercise power and perform functions; to carry on a business undertaking; and to make by-laws having the force of law, in relation to all or any of the matters specified in Schedule 2 of the Act.

In addition, ordinances could be made to allow the council to raise revenue by levying rates and imposing fees and charges, and to expend the monies of the council for the purposes of the council, including payment of the remuneration and allowances of members of the council. The council, by ordinance, could also enforce by-laws and punish persons committing offences against them.

To provide input to discussions on island matters, the council was empowered to consider and tender advice to the administrator concerning any matter affecting the government of the territory; and any matter could be brought before the council by a member of the council or, with the permission of the chairman of the council, by any other person or institution.

The governor-general could make ordinances for the peace, order, and good government of the territory and notice of the making of every ordinance was to be published in the Norfolk Island *Government Gazette*; unless the contrary intention appeared in an ordinance, it was to come into operation on the date of publication of the notice. Proposed ordinances were to be furnished by the minister, through the administrator, to the council for its consideration. If the council thought fit, it could make representations in writing to the administrator, and the administrator was required to forward the representation to the minister, together with his written observations (if any) that he thought fit to make in relation to the representation.

Where a copy of a proposed ordinance had been given to the council and the minister had received and considered the council's representations and any observations of the administrator, or a period of not less than 30 days had elapsed from the date of receipt of the proposed ordinance by council and the minister had not received any objections, the proposed ordinance could then be made by the governor-general. Ordinances would be laid before each House of Parliament within fifteen days instead of the thirty days allowed under the former Act, and if they were not so laid, the ordinance was void and of no effect.⁶⁰

Another significant change in the 1957 Act was the organisation of a different judicial system. The Supreme Court of Norfolk Island was constituted; it provided for a judge appointed in accordance with the Act, and it was to be a superior court of record. The governor-general appointed the judge, who could be removed from office by him in certain circumstances, but the judge's term of office was limited to the age of 65 years.

Provision was made in the Act for other courts and tribunals to be established by or under an ordinance, and the Court of Petty Sessions was constituted under this qualification. The High Court had jurisdiction, with such exceptions and subject to such conditions as were provided by ordinance, to hear and determine appeals from all judgements, decrees, orders, and sentences of the Supreme Court.

The *Norfolk Island Act 1957* was the government's response to the community to meet its demand for a "greater measure of autonomy" than it formerly had, and it arose as a direct result of the community's antagonism to the Customs Ordinance. An extended period of complex argument and compromise ensued before the council finally agreed to accept the draft Norfolk Island Council Ordinance, in which the new voting arrangement was incorporated at section 19(2). The 1957 Act was proclaimed on 1 April 1960 and the Norfolk Island Council Ordinance 1960, made on 7 April 1960, commenced one week later on 14 April when the subordinate legislation became law.⁶¹

In the lead-up to the 1960 legislation, the Progress Association had been a strident voice in the drive for more power in the management of local affairs: Newbald and Needham headed the campaign. The new legislation, however, had been agreed and accepted by the advisory council then in power, who were: W M Randall, president, and the councillors A S Bathie, N C Christian, L D Holloway, W T McCoy, R H H Nobbs and J D Patterson.

The election for the first Norfolk Island Council was held on 15 June 1960, but nominations for candidates were to be received by 1 June. Seventeen men and two women were nominated, and the eight candidates with the highest number of votes were to be declared councillors. The 2 June edition of *Norfolk News* announced that it would make space available for any candidate who wanted to present his/her policy. On that day a group of seven candidates stated their policy which proposed, in brief: "To restore to the citizens of Norfolk Island control over their domestic affairs"; to give council the "power to make laws" in Norfolk Island, and to "control" the "raising and spending of all revenue". Six of this group of seven were subsequently elected – councillors Needham, Newbold, Bailey, S E Nobbs, J F C Quintal and L V Nola, all apparently members of the Progress Association.

Three other candidates took advantage of the paper's offer of advertising space, one of whom, Mrs Kit Donkin, was elected; the eighth candidate chosen was F C Christian. It was a new council with a new policy.[62]

At the first meeting after the election Councillor Needham was chosen as president. It became clear soon after that the way forward would not be smooth. The administrator, R S Leydin, informed the department that at a special meeting held on 28 June the council had passed the following resolution.

> That this Council cannot accept the powers and functions set out in the Norfolk Island Council Ordinance 1960 whilst it contains the power of veto by the Administrator and involves pressure on the Council to raise more taxes. Furthermore this Council considers that the Ordinance cannot function satisfactorily unless it gives control over the public revenue of Norfolk Island to its citizens.

A detailed copy of council's objections to the 1960 Ordinance was conveyed to the authorities. The association argued that the 1957 Act and the foregoing Ordinance did not "meet the basic aspirations of the people" for their democratic rights, and in "no way" dealt with the 1955 petition to the Queen. They complained that the "major change in the constitution was not put to the people for approval . . ." and that it was "unacceptable in its present form". But the former council, with a different political point of view, had negotiated with Leydin and Hasluck and the Ordinance had been drafted "as discussed" with that council. The success of the group of six, known as "The Bloc", at the 1960 council election clearly indicated that it had the support of the majority of residents; this gave The Bloc the opportunity to aggressively promote its reform agenda.

In the copy of its objection sent to the administrator, probably formulated at the 5 July 1960 meeting, the council asked the minister to amend the legislation to give the council power to make laws for the island and to give complete control over the revenue raised locally. In addition, the council wanted "advisory powers" on all other matters such as "economies in management" and "complete freedom in its initiative concerning matters relating to policy for the Island's development". Members did not want "remote control from the mainland" over their domestic affairs.[63]

Incorporated in the council's main objection, however, was that the legislation did not "give the citizens control over the raising and spending of all revenue in Norfolk Island therefore there [was] taxation without representation through the Council"; the council wanted power to make laws that were of a "suitable and practical nature" in relation to the size of the community of 480 adults. Other issues appeared on the list of objections: overheads were too high and beyond the island's economic capacity; the Post Office and other administration establishments were inconveniently located at Kingston and the council requested that they be moved to a point closer to the centre of the island.

At the meeting of 5 July 1960, the council passed a resolution publishing its "Statement of Policy", with a resolution requesting that the minister "recognise and confirm agreement" to the statement; this was subsequently forwarded to the administrator. The first policy item listed was to achieve absolute control with regard to "raising and expenditure of all forms of revenue" on the island "to enable the will of the people to be the basis of authority". Other policies stated were to provide for education, medical care, the aged and needy, public services, freedom from unnecessary restrictions, the encouragement of settlers, tourism and other industry, and finally, "to be constantly on the watch for the less-conventional and most profitable ways of bringing wealth to the Island and its people".

The minister replied to this on 5 December 1960, indicating that the resolution added to the Statement of Policy requesting the government to "recognise and confirm agreement" to the policy was not clear and would require clarification.

One month later a council meeting of 10 January 1961 passed a resolution admonishing the minister. It stated that "the Minister [did] reply to Council's request that he recognise and confirm agreement to Council's policy . . . " The administrator passed the text of this resolution on to the minister on 25 January 1961. Leydin pointed out that the council was a "corporate body" and did not need the minister's approval to formulate a guide to its own activities; and in any case, the minister, "in as kind a way as may be", had already replied to the policy on 5 December 1960 and the several proposals made were "unacceptable and meaningless in their present form". Council's proposals were general, Leydin commented to the minister, and they were not accompanied by any explanation of them, any suggestions of the method which might be adopted to make them effective or any evidence to show that adoption of the proposals [was] in fact practical or wise having regard to the present resources and requirements of the Island's population". Leydin suggested the council be advised that the policy was being considered but that any proposal for the transfer of revenue "must be related to the works and services for the carrying out and the conduct in which the Council [was] prepared to accept responsibility".[64]

A report on the "Government of Norfolk Island" prepared by W H Scott, a special projects officer, on 10 March 1961, concluded that the department's analysis of the situation presented a "convincing argument" that the provisions for government were "reasonable and even generous", but the fact remained that the council, as the government's elected body, would not accept them. He was not optimistic about finding a solution to the unsatisfactory situation "other than a complete recasting of proposals" and suggested that "difficult questions" might possibly be settled "by direct negotiation".[65]

Succeeding departmental minutes agreed with Scott's assessment and suggested to P L Ryan, the acting administrator during Leydin's absence, that he be "as diplomatic as possible and endeavour to modify some of the hostile attitudes of the members of Council".[66]

Ryan commented in his letter of 24 March 1961 that he gained the impression Newbald's influence was "probably waning", but he informed the department that five of the councillors had "pledged to support each other" on an "all for one and one for all basis". There was some evidence to suggest that one or two members of The Bloc were "no longer convinced of the correctness of its cause but loyalty to a pledge prevented them from defecting". A special meeting held on 15 March, Ryan thought, had served a good purpose in that it provided an opportunity to air points of view that had been "submerged by The Bloc's persistent campaign to push its own point of view exclusively and avoid occasions where another viewpoint could be expressed".

On the same day and prior to his departure from Norfolk, Leydin wrote to the department outlining the probable reasons why the election of The Bloc had been so successful. The group was "very active" in its campaign: the members had organised frequent meetings, "how-to-vote" cards and others, as opposed to the lack of campaigning and organisation by their opponents. Other contributing factors to the result were the large number of nineteen candidates – which had the effect of dividing the opposition's support – the former council's suggestion that income tax be introduced, and the support from electors who were opposed to any change in the present system of government.

Two public meetings had been held since the June elections at which the council was criticised. At the second meeting, a motion was carried calling on the council to accept the government's proposals, but the majority was very small. A later by-election provided electors with their first opportunity to make a clear choice of alternatives. Both candidates issued circulars and stated their policies in the administration newspaper. R Westlake was a firm supporter of the group and its policy, but A S Bathie advocated acceptance of the governments' proposals. Bathie was elected.

The "obstacle" to progress, Leydin believed, was the council's wish to "have absolute control of public revenue while refusing to accept responsibility for the conduct of any of the public services or for doing any of the work financed by that revenue". He recommended that council be told "clearly and firmly" that its proposal to control all revenue, together with full legislative powers, "while leaving the conduct of all public services and the carrying out of all public works to the Administration [was] quite unrealistic and impracticable". Any transfer of authority would involve the acceptance of responsibility for the conduct of the activities transferred. Otherwise an impossible situation could arise, where policy instructions took no account of the feasibility of performance. Leydin suggested that a visit by the minister would be "beneficial".[67]

In its attempt to meet the council's demands, alternative forms of government were considered. The island could be given complete "self-government", but it was thought, an "insufficiency" of residents with ability and experience to control the full range of government functions would make it unworkable. If the system broke down, the Australian Government would "almost certainly" be obliged to take control again, probably at considerable expense. In assessing the situation, the department decided that the best way forward was to persevere with the present arrangement, but to make concessions to the council on some particular points. It was felt that there was "no better way" of working towards political self-sufficiency than by the residents, through their council, demonstrating their ability to control local affairs "progressively" until all desired powers were in their own hands. The minister endorsed the department's views and approved that a discussion be held between the council, the administrator, and senior officer of the department, with the object of securing sufficient modifications of council's views to enable a solution to be achieved.[68]

A background paper for use in the forthcoming discussions was prepared in which alternatives were suggested. The department favoured negotiation with the present council on the basis that "if some less objectional proposals [were] granted" the council would compromise by accepting responsibility for at least the basic development of the government's plan.

Another alternative considered was that a modified form of self-government could be "possible", working along the lines of the Northern Territory or the territory of Papua and New Guinea.⁶⁹

The 1961 council election, unfortunately for the government, did not achieve the hoped-for results. Councillors Needham, Newbald, Bailey, and Nobbs presented an electoral message with a "how-to-vote" pamphlet, both of which were issued three or four days before the election. A "spurious" poster, evidently printed in Australia, purporting to be Bathie's voting instructions and his support for the imposition of income tax, as well as an "untrue" statement about the administrator, was posted in many places during the night before the eve of the election. The administration did not know who was responsible for the poster or for its distribution. In the event, Bathie, who "vigorously supported" the administration's idea for local government, was defeated. A former president of the advisory council, W M Randall, a known opponent of any form of local government – including Newbald's ideas – was elected, as was resident R G Westlake, who defeated Greg Quintal. As a result, the nominal position was that the majority bloc had the support of seven councillors with Randall in "solitary and perhaps only partial" opposition. Leydin hoped that if it could be "got into the heads" of the majority councillors and their supporters that if they wished to have authority they must also accept responsibility, then it could be possible to find some way of working with the council.⁷⁰

As requested by the administrator, Hasluck went to the island on 9 August 1961 to try to improve the state of affairs between council and the authorities. A special meeting was held on 10 August. At the commencement of the meeting, president Needham proposed that it be held in committee "to avoid any misleading reports which [might] circulate and jeopardise council's work". All but Randall supported this motion. The minister intervened to say that he was willing to hear anything said in committee, but he would not speak at all in committee; he would, on the other hand, listen "very patiently". Councillors Needham, Newbald, and Bailey stated their position and policies at length while the minister paid attention. But when the meeting progressed to what decisions about governance should be made, Hasluck interrupted the proceedings to state his attitude to a closed meeting. From what he had heard, there was a variety of public opinion about administrative control of the island, and he felt that he should not enter on discussion on matters affecting the whole community at a closed meeting. The subject of a referendum was mentioned. The minister commented that he had "no objection" to this proposal, but the big problem undertaking a referendum was to frame the question in "such a simple way" that the answer you got was a true answer of the individual. The first essential was to isolate all the possibilities so that each person could choose what he really wanted.[71]

Towards the end of the meeting it was agreed that the task of council was to reduce to a precise form any amendments it wanted to make to the Ordinance and the Act, so that it would give to the people and to the parliament and draftsmen a clear understanding of the issues involved. It was suggested that the council did nothing but advise the administrator and scrutinise ordinances, or that it did what the 1960 Ordinance provided. A third option for a "satisfactory form of government" was stated by Needham at the 10 August meeting. In summary, the council considered that the "people should have control over their local revenue and the elected Council should have the power to make laws for the Island which were to be agreed by the Commonwealth Government which had a power of veto". The council wished to retain its existing advisory powers, but it felt that money could be saved and a more "efficient operation" achieved if the administrator was an ex-officio member of council. In this way a single tier form of government would be instituted.[72]

Major General R H Wordsworth, the next administrator, arrived at Norfolk on 9 June 1962. In reply to a memorandum from Wordsworth, Hasluck agreed with him that the "best approach" to the current problem would be to draft an ordinance and, if necessary, an amendment to the Act, expressing what the government was prepared to do, and at the same time attempting to obtain the concurrence of the Norfolk Island Council on its terms. Hasluck did not want to go on "splitting the people of the Island" into factions, and he thought it was important to be sure that there was no significant group leading a movement away from the decisions a substantial body of the people preferred. The minister did not want to leave either side in the argument feeling that it had been "defeated or abandoned".[73]

A department submission to the minister, dated 26 September 1962, set out the administrator's proposals for new powers for the Norfolk Island Council. One consideration put forward by Wordsworth, regarding the type of council, contemplated a council patterned on the administrators' councils of the Northern Territory and Papua and New Guinea, but he apparently rejected this idea because "in those territories members of the Administrators' Councils were appointed, not elected, and members – though drawn from the legislatures – constituted only part of those legislatures".

The minister directed that the administrator be informed of his recommendations in reply to Wordsworth's memorandum of 17 August. Some of Hasluck's main proposals advised that the existing council be constituted an administrator's council; actions decided upon and permitted to be taken by the administrator were to be taken by the administrator with the advice of the council; and if the administrator did not accept council's advice he was to report his and council's reasons to the minister. Wherever practicable, proposed ordinances were to be considered by the administrator and council before detailed drafting, except when it was necessary that an urgent ordinance be made without prior reference to the council. Council had no power to direct the administrator, and local revenue was to be spent only in accordance with estimates provided by the council.

With regard to the power of the council to hold a referendum, the minister recommended that power be given "to hold referendums including referendums which might be sought by the Council", but the decision upon taking referendums and their terms was to be subject to the approval of the minister.[74]

Following the above recommendations approved by the minister, further negotiations regarding the Norfolk Island Ordinance were, apparently, in abeyance. Very little information on this subject appeared in the island newspaper, *Norfolk News*, until 7 November 1963. On that day the editor published a report stating that the council had "unanimously" passed a motion of thanks to the minister for territories for his assistance in seeing the Bill on amendments to the *Norfolk*

Island Act passed through all stages of parliament. The council had accepted the *Norfolk Island Bill 1963* at its meeting on 5 November. The Bill had removed the restricted local-body form of council with its rating and further tax-raising powers to cover the cost of a double administration. Speaking in support of the Bill in the House, E G Whitlam, deputy leader of the opposition, agreed with the proposition that the population of Norfolk could not support "two-tier" systems of government. In his address to parliament, Hasluck said that under the new system, with the administrator being a member of the council, the advice of council became the decision, except on rare occasions when the minister countermanded the decision of council. In concluding his address, Hasluck emphasised that the changes were made at the "express wish of the Norfolk Island Council", which assured him that it was voicing the wishes of the people.

Although the council "no longer had the power to carry out the functions of a local government nature, the people through the expansion of the advisory powers of the council [would] have a fuller opportunity to express [its] views on all matters affecting the government of the Territory" and he commended the Bill to the House.[75]

Soon after, the *Norfolk Island Act* (No. 101 of 1963) was assented to on 1 November 1963. The Norfolk Island Ordinance 1964 was later amended to provide for the Norfolk Island Council to consist of the administrator and eight elected members, and the office of president became the president of committees. Part 5, under "meetings of Council", section 55 stated that the administrator was to be the chairman of the council and preside at all council meetings; questions arising at a council meeting were to be decided by a majority vote, and each member of the council had a deliberative vote. In the event of an equality of votes, the chairman had a casting vote. This Ordinance was gazetted on 23 April 1964 and proclaimed on 1 July 1964. At the first council meeting on 12 May 1964 the administrator, in taking his office of chairman of the council, expressed his appreciation for the work done by Councillor Needham over the last years as president of the council. The council became an advisory council, but the system, Wordsworth cautioned, would work only if council and the administrator had confidence in each other and worked with "full cooperation".[76]

Tourism: looking to the future

A vital part of Norfolk Island's post-war reconstruction of the local economy was the development of the tourism trade, made possible, largely, by the building of the aerodrome. The potential for tourist growth looked promising, but it was hindered by a lack of modern accommodation. The existing boarding houses were too few and in need of renovation, and post-war shortages of building materials impeded repairs to the old, as well as construction of new, accommodation.

With the future of the island in mind, in July 1946 Administrator Alex Wilson submitted a proposal to the minister for external territories for the erection of a hotel on Norfolk to accommodate approximately 40 guests. The design was to be modern, built in local timber and included all essential services. He informed the advisory council of his action, and the council expressed its support, further suggesting that the liquor laws be amended to allow for a licensed hotel and the sale of liquor under government control. The hotel was to be operated by the administration.[77]

Wilson held out hope until 1950 that the administration's hotel would be built, in which year the department informed him that construction of a government-owned hotel in the territory at that time was "not favoured". Government policy was for the operation of such establishments to be done by private enterprise. It did, however, agree to consider the question of licences to guesthouses and clubs to cover the serving of liquor with meals and/or during restricted hours.[78]

The department sought council's views on the matter of extending facilities for the purchase and consumption of liquor on the island. In a memorandum of 12 May 1950, the administrator advised the department that certain guesthouse proprietors had approached him and suggested that an ordinance should be made to regulate local guesthouses. The deputation pointed out that a person in possession of any class of building could set himself up in the guesthouse business. It was alleged that some buildings provided "only one primitive bath and only one earth closet" for the use of guests and staff of both sexes, and some proprietors accepted a number of guests "far in excess" of the accommodation available, a "quarter of these" being for beds on verandahs "without even providing a dressing room for their use". This state of affairs, it was argued, would lead to "severe criticism" and affect the future prosperity of tourism.

The deputation suggested that guesthouses should be licensed, "that the licence should specify the number of guests who might be accepted in particular guesthouses, that not less than two bathrooms and two lavatories of approved standard should be provided". Lighting, furniture, furnishings, and other facilities were to be of "a reasonable standard". The proprietors thought the laws should state "definite standards" for new buildings, and approval should be given before construction could commence. Registration would depend on compliance with the regulations. Some proprietors invested capital and improved their premises, but others were not prepared to invest on a long-term basis. These people understood that they would be out of business once modern lodgings were available, and they merely wished to get a quick return while there was still a demand. Wilson suggested that the deputation prepare a "detailed scheme" of appropriate regulations, which he would furnish to the minister.[79]

Over the next four years other local issues took up the time and energy of the advisory council, and discussion about tourist accommodation was put aside. In August/September 1954, however, the advisory council again discussed the subject, and council arrived at a "detailed scheme" for an ordinance for regulation of boarding houses and boarding house regulations. At the meeting on 1 September 1954, the scheme was tabled and a resolution to accept the new law, subject to the stated amendments, was carried unanimously.

In the *Annual Report* for 1956 the administrator, Brigadier H B Norman, announced that due to the "importance" of the tourism trade to the economy of the territory, the Boarding Houses Ordinance 1955 had been passed and came into force on 5 May 1955. The Ordinance made provision for registration of proprietors of guesthouses catering for guests in excess of five, registration being contingent upon the provision of guest accommodation of a certain minimum standard. On that day there were seven guesthouses operating, but proprietors of only two of these were registered by 30 June 1956. Other registrations followed soon after to cater for the growing numbers of visitors, and in 1960 the figure rose to 978 persons. An ordinance for the sale of liquor was passed on the same day as the regulation for boarding houses. The Liquor Ordinance of 1960 commenced on 5 May, thus enabling a licensed residential hotel to be opened at Kingston. There were, in addition, five guesthouses in operation.

Associated with the improvements in visitor accommodation, the introduction of a regular, same-day civil air service from both New Zealand and Sydney in the late 1940s marked the start of what was to become the island's chief source of income. Growth was uneven up to 1960, but with the development of the tourism trade, the number of visitors grew steadily up to 1980. The regulations controlling the tourism industry from 1960 were to work to the advantage of the residents and the preservation of the island itself in later years.

With the commencement of the new legislation in the mid-1960s and a return to the day-to-day concerns of the community, issues relating to the social welfare of the Islanders came to the fore. Thirty years before, two matters had been raised that appeared to be the first of a number of suggestions for the introduction of insurance schemes to cover old age pensions and workers compensation. While the Islanders had requested the administration to assist in providing this form of protection from 1935, no legislation had been forthcoming.

Early references to the foregoing, however, did not emanate from the advisory council; they were prompted by the local newspaper and the residents. An editorial in the *Norfolk Island Times* of 19 April 1935, which reported the executive council meeting of 3 April, chided members of the council for not approaching Canberra when they had the opportunity, when the council was "so anxious for relief of the elderly folks". It seemed extraordinary that council did not "think" of asking for old age pensions. The next month the *Times* published a letter from a correspondent, "Sapientissimuss", who pointed out the danger of accidents at work and therefore a need for an accident insurance policy to cover workplace injuries.[80]

Both of these ideas arose on many occasions before legislation was finally enacted. It seemed the constant problem – that the island revenue was insufficient to fund an insurance scheme – was partly responsible for the lack of action. Although the administration accepted some responsibility for support for aged and injured workers, the government's reaction was to provide financial assistance when they considered it was required. This was known as the "ex gratia policy".[81]

From 1964 there was a change in attitude towards local affairs. After the acrimony of previous years and a cooling-off period for over-heated tempers, the general atmosphere in the community seemed conducive to reconsideration of old issues, as well as to the addition of new measures for social services.

Aware of the benefits received by Australians through their welfare programs, certain island residents began to press for the establishment of similar systems in Norfolk Island. There were a number of letters sent by individuals to the *Norfolk News* providing information about various schemes and promoting the value of such initiatives. High on the list of the community's priorities were hospital and medical benefits, child endowment, widows' pensions, and unemployment relief, as well as others. In addition to these, there was a move to implement another way to identify ownership of land, the Torrens title system. But arguments about the cost as against the benefit of such schemes continued to be debated for a considerable number of years, and thus retarded important reform.

Chapter 6

Nimmo and After

By letters patent dated 15 May 1975, Sir John Angus Nimmo CBE was appointed by the Federal Government as a royal commissioner to inquire into, and make recommendations on, the future status of Norfolk Island, its constitutional relationship to Australia, and the most appropriate form of administration for the island if its constitutional position were changed. These very wide terms of reference were given some specificity by requiring the commissioner to extend his enquiry, and to take into account, the following enumerated topics, among others:

1. The interests of Norfolk Island residents and the historical rights of the Pitcairn settlers, arising from their settlement in 1856;
2. Norfolk Island's legal position as a territory of Australia;
3. Whether social security, pensions, health, compensation, and other benefits should be provided at levels similar to those which Australian citizens enjoy, and the capacity and willingness of the island to pay through taxation or other imposts for the provision of those benefits;

4. The extent to which Norfolk Island has been and is now being used to provide a base for activities (e.g. income tax, gift duty, and death duty avoidance or evasion) which are harmful to the interests of Australia or of other countries;
5. Conditions for permanent entry into the island community;
6. The need for adequate communication between the island and Australia, and the rest of the world; and
7. The need for adequate law enforcement and judicial machinery.[1]

In relation to the first principal matter within the terms of reference, namely the future status of Norfolk Island and its constitutional relationship to Australia, the commission recommended that:

> The Commonwealth Government decide as soon as practicable and announce its decision on whether it proposes to abandon Norfolk Island completely or to continue to accept responsibility for maintaining it as a viable community.

> That, if the Commonwealth Government decides not to abandon Norfolk Island completely then for at least five years the status of the Island and its constitutional relationship to Australia remain that of a Territory of the Commonwealth of Australia.[2]

In relation to the second principal matter, namely the most appropriate form of administration for Norfolk Island if its constitutional position were changed, the commission's recommendations were as follows:

That residents of Norfolk Island be included in the electorate of Canberra in the Australian Capital Territory for the purpose of giving them representation in the Commonwealth Parliament.

That the present Norfolk Island Council be abolished and replaced by an incorporated body to be known as the "Norfolk Island Territory Assembly".

That legislative and executive powers be granted to the Assembly in respect of an enumerated list of matters, including:

> roads, footpaths and bridges; drainage; sewerage and sanitation; disposal of garbage and trade waste; recreation areas; pasturage on commons, livestock; pounds; pests and noxious weeds; cemeteries; guest houses; electricity supply; water supply; lighterage; places of public entertainment; promotion of tourism; omnibuses and taxis; sale and distribution of food stuffs and beverages; repair or demolition of dangerous buildings; new buildings and the alteration of buildings; advertising hoardings; fires and the prevention of fires; road traffic; street lighting; prevention and suppression of nuisances; trading hours; street stalls; raising revenue for the Assembly's budget; coastlines, foreshores; wharves and jetties; fishing; slaughtering of stock; domestic animals and birds; storage of petroleum products; firearms; museums, memorials and libraries; motor vehicles and road traffic; forestry and related activities; radio and television; noxious trades; markets and weigh bridges; carters and hawkers;

quarrying; maintenance of rolls; telephone services; postal services; customs services; philatelic activities; immigration, with a right of appeal to the Federal Minister by any person aggrieved; registrations (births, deaths, marriages, companies, motor vehicles, dogs etc) which are at present handled by the Administration; internal audits; the undertaking of business activities and contracts with respect to any of the matters specified above.[3]

The majority of these matters were of a state or local government nature. For the purposes of raising revenue for its budget, the assembly should take over those operations at present yielding revenue to the administration other than those relating to hospital and medical services.

The commission concluded that the assembly should not be given the power to borrow money but be given the right to apply to the Commonwealth Grants Commission for financial assistance.

Further recommendations included:

- "That the Administrator possess no power of veto over the Assembly's legislative and executive responsibilities, nor hold any membership or office of the Assembly".
- "That the Commonwealth continue to exercise all governmental powers not shown above as being specifically conferred upon the Assembly and, in particular, retain all powers over all land in the Island".
- The commission also recommended that "the performance of the Assembly be reviewed by the Commonwealth after

five years and consideration be then given to the question of increasing the powers of the Assembly".
- Further, "that the Commonwealth Government in the light of this report lay down a clear set of policies to be followed in the administration of Norfolk Island", particularly in respect of the following:
  - land development and ownership;
  - the airport;
  - taxation;
  - health services;
  - law;
  - social security;
  - education;
  - transport to and from the mainland;
  - government buildings and historical sites; and
  - tourism generally.

Further recommendations were:

- That the Commonwealth consult the Assembly on all matters which hold particular relevance to Norfolk Island and where practicable give the Island opportunity of sending representatives to meetings of international bodies whose deliberations may specifically affect the Island.
- That when the supply of legal draftsmen permits, a particular draftsman in the Legislative Drafting Division of the Attorney-General's Department be appointed and instructed to give priority to the drafting of Ordinances relating to the Island.[4]

In relation to the topic "The present and probable development of the economy of Norfolk Island", the commission made the following recommendations:

- That the number of tourists visiting the Island should not exceed 20,000 in any one year.
- That the plan for the restoration and maintenance of historic building sites be maintained.
- That the practice of fouling the coastline by emptying untreated garbage into the sea be terminated and replaced by a proper garbage disposal system.
- That cattle grazing in government-owned pine forest areas be prohibited and that such areas be reafforested.
- That constant care be exercised in the setting of custom duties in the Island to ensure that low-duty shopping remains available.
- That higher standards of town planning and building control be introduced and implemented.

One of the most important recommendations related to social security and related matters. The commission recommended "that all social security, all pension and all medical, hospital and other health benefits dispensed by the Commonwealth Government be extended to residents of Norfolk Island".[5]

With respect to education:

- The onus be on the Commonwealth Government to ensure that the educational facilities available in Norfolk Island are at the same standard as those obtaining in mainland territories; and that the present close and developed

association with the New South Wales Department of Education be allowed to continue.
- That Commonwealth legislation with regards to workers compensation be extended immediately to Norfolk Island.
- That citizens in Norfolk Island be made liable to the same levels of taxation and other imposts as apply in the Australian Capital Territory.[6]

In relation to "conditions for permanent entry into the Island community", the recommendations included:

- That steps be taken immediately to expedite the making of the amendments to the Immigration Ordinance which were approved by the Norfolk Island Council and the Minister in 1974.
- That, in connection with land sales to persons not resident in the Island, such land sales should be permitted:
  (a) if it can be established that the intending purchaser is a bona fide and prospective settler in the Island;

  (b) if no person in Norfolk Island is ready, willing and able to purchase the property at the sale price;

  (c) if the intending vendor renounces his residency after the sale; and

  (d) if the number of people entering the Island as a result of such sale would not exceed the number leaving.

- That the notion that formal priority should be given to Pitcairn descendants and their spouses, when considering residency applications, be abandoned as being incompatible with the Racial Discrimination Act 1975.

In relation to the need for adequate communications between the island and Australia, and the rest of the world, the recommendations included the following:

- That Qantas be relieved of responsibility for the Sydney-Norfolk Island route as soon as practicable.
- That only one airline operator take over from Qantas; that operator to be in a position to ensure continuity of service by having available suitable numbers of aircraft and be able to integrate the Norfolk Island route with other routes so that tariffs can be kept to a minimum and high standards of service be maintained, without subsidisation by the Commonwealth Government.
- That the Commonwealth Government finance and control the Island's airport and related activities.
- That the Federal Government arrange for one shipping line to be assured of the Sydney-Norfolk Island business subject to freight rates being carefully controlled.[8]

In relation to the need for adequate law enforcement and judicial machinery, the recommendations included the following:

- That non-law-enforcement activities of the police force be severed and handed over to Administration personnel.
- That laws of the Island be updated and consolidated as soon as possible, and be reviewed as part of any review

entrusted to the Law Reform Commission of the laws of all Australian Territories.
- That Island Magistrates, in addition to Supreme Court Judges, be empowered to grant bail.
- That the law library of the Island be supplemented by the addition of more works of reference.
- That adequate Court staffing arrangements be provided.
- That in order to give effect to the implications of the decision in the Berwick case, section 14 of the Norfolk Island Act 1957–1963 be amended to provide for all Commonwealth legislation, past or future, affecting Australia generally to be henceforth applicable to Norfolk Island unless the contrary is expressly stated.[9]

The report of the royal commissioner was delivered to the governor-general on 15 October 1976. It eventually led to the Norfolk Island Bill 1978, which became the *Norfolk Island Act 1979*. Royal assent to the 1979 Act was given on 30 May 1979. During the intervening period in December 1977, responsibility for Norfolk Island affairs was switched from the ministry of administrative affairs (the minister of which was Senator the Honourable R G Withers) to the new ministry of home affairs, the portfolio minister, for which was the Honourable R J Ellicott QC. The period from October 1976 to May 1979 – 32 months – saw a very active community movement in opposition, to the thrust of Nimmo's recommendations.

That opposition – chiefly, but not entirely, due to the activities of the Norfolk Island Council – included lobbying both in Canberra and on the island, media releases, and engagement of knowledgeable third parties, included but not limited to the United Nations Association of Australia.

For example, on 7 June 1977 a conference was held in Norfolk Island to discuss the extent to which the recommendations of the Nimmo Commission should be carried into effect.[10] The meeting included Senator Withers, Mr Ellicott, eight (being the whole) of the councillors of the Norfolk Island Council, officials such as the senior private secretary to the minister for administrative services and the private secretary to the attorney-general, and which meeting was broadcast. At that meeting, which took some two and a half hours, was discussed the proposal that Islanders be permitted and indeed required to vote in a Canberra electorate.

Broadly speaking, the attitude of the councillors present was hostile to reception of the recommendations as they stood.

The council sought a referendum of the electors of Norfolk Island on the issues arising from the Nimmo report. The views of the Norfolk Island Council on the Nimmo report commenced by referring to "two major errors of fact".[11] These were said to be "so large, that whatever attitude is taken to any of the report's major recommendations, it cannot be supported by the reasons given by the author and must be examined afresh". The second major error was asserted to be Nimmo's finding that Queen Victoria did not in fact "give" Norfolk Island to the Pitcairners. The document on this issue made the following points:

> On the contrary, she created Norfolk Island as a distinct and separate settlement for [the Pitcairners], and instructed her governor to preserve all the Pitcairn ways including

self-government. As a result, Island leaders met with Governor General Denison to frame the "thirty-nine laws" and ensure that real executive, legislative and judicial powers were left on the Island.

The council's remarks on this topic continued as follows:

> This does not necessarily mean that Australia's authority over the Island is displaced by those rights. It does mean however that that authority should be exercised at all times with the history and purposes of the Island firmly in mind. The Island is no more "part of the Commonwealth" in its history or its society than Papua was".[12]

The rights of residents to take the principal part in informing the island's political future was the chief concern of the council. Councils' remarks were predicated on the common understanding that there would be major tax and other imposts superimposed on the island's economy, and that the likely result of this would be an increase in the cost to tourists visiting Norfolk Island, and therefore a decline in the island's competitiveness with other tourist destinations. For those and other reasons, the council believed that the Nimmo report was not a sound document. Its importance lay in the impetus it brought to the island for change and further political development. The subjects covered by the report included most of the elements to be considered in looking at the island's political future.

Turning to the specific recommendations about federal voting, the council's attitude was as follows:

They opposed the proposal that the Islanders should be permitted and indeed required to vote in a Canberra electorate. That had always been a bone of contention between the Commonwealth and Norfolk Island. The fear of Norfolk Island representatives, whether in the Council or in other spheres, was that inclusion in a Federal electorate would not advance democracy for the Island. This was because the inclusion of the Island in a Canberra electorate would amount to "sheer tokenism" in that it would never be possible for Norfolk Islanders as a discrete group to overbear the electoral impact of a fully sized electorate. It would also yield a spurious impression of democracy.[13]

To the same effect, it had always been the case that Norfolk Islanders would not be subject to federal laws being applied to the island in toto. This had been a feature of the *Norfolk Island Act* of 1913, and was a feature of all subsequent governmental arrangements for the island until 2015. Further, there are indications in the earlier papers of the nineteenth century about the unsuitability of a wholesale importation of federal (or earlier, New South Wales) laws being recognised to be inappropriate for Norfolk Island.

The next most important recommendation was that federal compensation, law, and social security provision should be extended to the island. The councillors who addressed that issue expressed grave concerns about the economic impact on the island, and the "knock on" impact on the tourism industry. The council was agreeable to the principle that provision should be made for benefits of that kind, but that they should be effected by local island legislation, to take into account the island's specific circumstances.[14]

As noted above, the recommendations of the royal commission included a recommendation that the island's residents should be reflected in the island's legal position as a territory of Australia, and that its constitutional relationship was informed by the Berwick case, in which the High Court of Australia sought to clarify the issue of whether Norfolk Island was "part of" the Commonwealth, or rather, bore some other relation to the Commonwealth.[15]

By 8 May 1978, following further consideration by the Federal Government of the report of the royal commission, a major policy announcement on the island's future was made. By this stage, Senator Withers was no longer the minister for home affairs. He was replaced in that capacity by Mr Ellicott.

The central points of the press release of 8 May 1978 were as follows:

(a) The Federal Government was prepared over a period of time to move towards a substantial measure of self-government for the island and was also of the view that although Norfolk Island was a part of Australia and would remain so, that did not require Norfolk Island to be regulated by the same laws as regulate "other parts of Australia".

(b) The present situation under which laws of the Australian Parliament only applied to the island if special provision was made in the particular law would continue.

(c) The Federal Government would see if the island could develop an appropriate form of government involving its elected representatives under which the revenue necessary to sustain that government would be raised internally under its own system of law.

(d) An economic feasibility study would be commissioned.

(e) A statutory social security scheme should be established.

(f) The present Norfolk Island Council be abolished, and that instead there be an incorporated body to be known as the "Norfolk Island Legislative Assembly", with power to pass laws for the peace, order and good government of the island and with complete legislative power and executive control over a wide and specified list of matters, subject to a right of veto by the administrator in respect of education, immigration, customs services, and fishing in view of their particular sensitivity and national importance.

(g) The assembly would have major financial powers. The government believes that if the measures outlined are taken they will be a major step toward a form of self-government for the island. Consideration would be given to increasing the areas of the assembly's powers and executive responsibilities no later than five years after its incorporation.

(h) No decision would be taken on the question of representation in the Commonwealth Parliament until after consultations had been held with the legislative assembly.

(i) Commonwealth legislation with regard to workers compensation should not be extended to the island provided that a comprehensive accident insurance scheme satisfactory to the government and the legislative assembly was implemented.

(j) Steps should be taken to finalise and adopt environmental planning legislation with special arrangements for the Mt Pitt reserve area and other environmentally sensitive areas.

(k) "In all the circumstances and having regard to the decisions [the Federal Government] has made, a Referendum should not be held".[16]

The debate between the competing world views of the federal minister and the councillors of the Norfolk Island Council was exemplified and was the particular focus of a meeting held on 26 March 1979 in Sydney. As noted, by this stage the Honourable R J Ellicott QC was the minister for home affairs, and in attendance at the meeting with him were Councillors Blucher, Bennett, Buffett, McIntyre, McKenzie, Nunn, Quintal, and Snell. The administrator, Mr D V O'Leary, and officials, namely Messrs McCasker, Syrette, Ilyk, and Holmes.[17] At that meeting the focus of attention was on proposed amendments to the Bill as it stood before the House of Representatives. In particular, the form which amendments to the recitals at the beginning of the Bill (the preamble) should take. These were inserted in the Bill as it stood in the parliament and as subsequently enacted. That was doubtless as a counterweight to the council's pursuit of a solution based on Article 73 of the UN Charter. At the meeting on 26 March 1979 the following passage is recorded:

> Minister: I don't think you will find it difficult to recall what I say. I said I would look at certain things and I have done that.
>
> The Preamble: If you wanted to read like Article 73 you will have to chase it. I will hand you some recitals to go into the Bill that I have not yet presented to the government but which I am prepared to recommend to them. I believe they go a long way to satisfy what some of you are troubled about . . . I will hand you some pages of Preamble. It is an attempt to satisfy the aspiration of the island. They are taken extensively from the recitals in the 1913 Act and there are further ones typed at the end. I will hand around a further page with another clause which I am still considering. I do not want it taken as final. I am thinking that we could add at the end something like this: "And to provide a mechanism in this Act whereby following such consideration further powers may be conferred". Basically what I have done is to be consistent with what I have been saying, to accept the relation of the Pitcairn people with Norfolk Island.[18]

The amendments to the preamble which were circulated at that meeting were as follows:

And whereas the residents of Norfolk Island include descendants of the settlers from Pitcairn Island; And whereas the Parliament recognises the special relationship of the said descendants with Norfolk Island and their desire to preserve their traditions and culture; And whereas the Parliament considers it to be desirable and to be the wish of the people of Norfolk Island that Norfolk Island achieve, over a period of time, internal self-government as a Territory under the authority of the Commonwealth and, to that end, to provide, amongst other things, for the establishment of a representative Legislative Assembly and other separate political and administrative institutions on Norfolk Island; And whereas the Parliament intends that within a period of 5 years after the coming into operation of this Act consideration will be given of extending the powers conferred by or under this Act on the Legislative Assembly and the other political and administrative institutions of Norfolk Island and that provision be made in this Act to enable the results of such consideration to be implemented; Be it therefore enacted by the Queen, and the Senate and the House of Representatives of the Commonwealth of Australia . . .

The *Norfolk Island Act 1979* was, as noted above, assented to on 30 May 1979, and the date of commencement was 7 August 1979 for some of the provisions and the date of assent for the remainder. The scope of the legislative powers conferred by the Act were wide. Subsection 19(1) of the Act conferred legislative power on the legislative assembly, with the assent of the administrator or the governor-general, as the case may be, to make laws for the peace, order, and good governance of the territory.

However, there were carve-outs as follows:

> The Assembly's powers did not extend to the making of laws authorising the acquisition of property otherwise than on just terms, authorising the raising or maintaining of any naval, military or airforce or authorising the coining of money. Finally, and not in the Act in its original form, the Assembly did not have power to permit or have the effect of permitting (whether subject to conditions or not), the form of intentional killing of another called euthanasia (which includes mercy killing) or the assisting of a person to terminate his or her life.

These powers were obviously very wide, and their effect was not confined to matters falling within Schedules 2 and 3 to the Act, but Schedule 2 set out an enumerated list of powers which the assembly had and which were subject to the approval or assent of the administrator. Schedule 3 set out other matters, which had effect subject to the approval of the federal minister.

Schedule 2 was a long and enumerated list of powers which were in broadly similar terms to the recommendations of the royal commission, and these were extended during the life of the legislative assembly by Statutory Rules 1981 (No. 153) as amended by 1984 (No. 33), 1985 (No. 173), 1989 (No. 268), and 1992 (No. 164). Therefore the powers of the legislative assembly were significantly enhanced during the life of the assembly. Similarly, for Schedule 3 matters, Statutory Rules 1989 (No. 268) extended the powers of the legislative assembly during the life of the assembly.

In their final form, Schedules 2 and 3 were as follows:

Schedule 2

1. The raising of revenues for purposes of matters specified in this Schedule.
2. Public moneys of the territory (other than the raising of revenue).
3. Surface transport (including road safety, traffic control, carriers, vehicle registration, and the licensing of drivers).
4. Roads, footpaths, and bridges.
5. Street lighting.
6. Water supply.
7. Electricity supply.
8. Drainage and sewerage.
9. Garbage and trade waste.
10. Primary production.
11. The slaughtering of livestock.
12. Domestic animals (including birds).
13. Public pounds.
14. Pests and noxious weeds.
15. Recreation areas.
16. Cemeteries.

. . .

18. Fire prevention and control.
19. Quarrying.
20. Building control (including the repair or demolition of dangerous buildings).
21. Advertising hoardings.
22. The prevention and suppression of nuisances.

23. Noxious trades.
24. Gases and hydrocarbon fuels.
25. Firearms.
26. Explosives and dangerous substances.
27. Tourism.
28. Places of public entertainment.
29. Boarding houses and hotels.
30. Museums, memorials, and libraries.
31. Foodstuffs and beverages (including alcoholic liquor).
32. Trading hours.
33. Markets and street stalls.
34. Hawkers.
35. Radio and television.
36. Postal services.
37. Coastlines, foreshores, wharves, and jetties.
38. The transporting of passengers or goods to and from ships.
39. The maintenance of rolls of residents of the territory.

...

41. The registration of births, deaths, and marriages.
42. Matters in respect of which duties, powers, functions, or authorities are expressly imposed or conferred on executive members by or under laws in force in the territory other than a matter that relates to immigration or the operation of the *Immigration Act 1980* of the territory.
43. Public service of the territory.
44. Public works.
45. Lotteries, betting, and gaming.
46. Civil defence and emergency services.
47. Territory archives.
48. The provision of telecommunications services (within the

meaning of the *Telecommunications Act 1989*) and the prescribing of rates of charge for those services.
49. Branding and marking of livestock.
50. Pasturage and enclosure of animals.
51. Registration of bulls.
52. Bees and apiaries.
53. Exportation of fish and fish products from the territory.
54. Livestock diseases (other than quarantine).
55. Plant and fruit diseases (other than quarantine).
56. Water resources.
57. Energy planning and regulation.
58. Fences.
59. Business names.
60. Navigation, including boating.
61. Price and cost indexes.
62. Fundraising from the public for non-commercial purposes, and associations registered for fundraising of that type.
63. Administration of estates and trusts.
64. Census and statistics.
65. Inquiries and administrative reviews.
66. Registration of medical practitioners and dentists.
67. Public health (other than dangerous drugs, within the meaning of the Dangerous Drugs Ordinance 1927 of the territory, psychotropic substances quarantine).
68. Mercantile law (including sale or lease of goods, charges, and liens on goods or crops; supply of services).
69. Law relating to the interpretation of enactments.
70. Civil legal proceedings by and against the administration of the territory.
71. Official flag and emblem, and public seal, of the territory.

72. Fees or taxes imposed by the following enactments of the territory: Absentee Landowners Levy Ordinance 1976; *Cheques (Duty) Act 1983*; *Departure Fee Act 1980*; *Financial Institutions Levy Act 1985*; *Fuel Levy Act 1987*; Public Works Levy Ordinance 1976.
73. Protection of birds.
74. Matters incidental to or consequential on the execution of executive authority.
75. Remuneration, allowances, and other entitlements in respect of services of members of the legislative assembly, members of the executive council and other offices in or in connection with the legislative assembly that can be held only by members of the assembly.
76. Prices and rent control.
77. Printing and publishing.
78. Public utilities.
79. Housing.
80. Community and cultural affairs.
81. Industry (including forestry and timber, pastoral, agricultural, building, and manufacturing).
82. Mining and minerals (excluding uranium or other prescribed substances within the meaning of the *Atomic Energy Act 1953* and regulations under that Act as in force from time to time), within all the land of the territory above the low-water mark.
83. Provision of rural, industrial, and home finance credit and assistance.
84. Scientific research.
85. Legal aid.
86. Corporate affairs.

87. Censorship.
88. Child, family, and social welfare.
89. Regulation of businesses and professions.
90. The legal profession.
91. Maintenance of law and order and the administration of justice.
92. Correctional services.
93. Private law.

Schedule 3

1. Fishing.
2. Customs (including the imposition of duties).
3. Immigration.
4. Education.
5. Human quarantine.
6. Animal quarantine.
7. Plant quarantine.
8. Labour and industrial relations, employees' compensation, and occupational health and safety.
9. Movable cultural heritage objects.
10. Social security.

It may be thought that the amplitude of the powers of legislation and exercise of executive authority enumerated in Schedules 2 and 3 were so wide that the assembly was effectively in charge of all aspects of those activities. This, however, would be a mistake. The Schedules are based upon regulations made in respect of the Northern Territory: Northern Territory (Self-Government) Regulations 1978 (Regulation 4). There are numerous heads of power in Schedules 2 and 3 that would not be effectively exercisable by the Norfolk Island Legislative Assembly or the Norfolk Island Executive Council. There is much overlap and duplication in the framing of the items of Schedules 2 and 3. Many activities of the Federal Government would in practice impinge upon the powers of the legislative assembly. If there were to arise an inconsistency between a federal law and a Norfolk Island law made in accordance with one or more of the items in Schedules 2 and 3, the federal law would prevail. To this extent, the Schedules would be a dead letter. Further, section 23 of the *Norfolk Island Act 1979* gives the governor-general the power to disallow laws made by the legislative assembly and assented to by the administrator. This power of disallowance is unqualified in its terms, save that there is a time limit of six months. For these and other reasons, the assembly would have had a much more constrained ambit of operation than the Schedules seem to indicate.

It is true beyond any doubt that Norfolk Island was closely supervised by federal authorities over time. During the period between 1991 and 2004, the following federal inquiries affected the island.

- March 1991 – Islands in the sun: the legal regimes of Australia's external territories and the Jervis Bay territory. House of Representatives Standing Committee on legal and constitutional affairs.
- March 1999 – Territorial limits. Norfolk Island's *Immigration Act* and human rights. Human Rights and Equal Opportunity Commission (report to the federal attorney-general).
- March 1999 – Island to islands. Communication with

Australia's external territories. Report of Joint Standing Committee on the National Capital and External Territories (JSCNCET).
- August 1999 – Report on the Norfolk Island Amendment Bill 1999. Report of the Senate Standing Committee on legal and constitutional legislation.
- July 2001 – In the pink or in the red? Health services of Norfolk Island. Report of JSCNCET.
- October 2001 – JSCNCET inquiry into Norfolk Island electoral matters (lapsed on dissolution of the 39th Parliament).
- June 2002 – Report of inquiry into Norfolk Island electoral matters. Report of JSCNCET.
- December 2003 – Report of inquiry into regional aviation services in Australia and to transport links to major populated islands. Report of House of Representatives Standing Committee on transport and regional services.
- December 2003 – *Quis Custodiet Ipsos Custodes?: Inquiry into Governance on Norfolk Island*. JSCNCET.

The defeat of the Norfolk Island Amendment Bill 1999 was followed by its replacement in the next parliament by a referral to the JSCNCET for further consideration of proposed changes.

The governance inquiry's report of December 2003 involved a root and branch challenge to the understanding on which the *Norfolk Island Act 1979* was based. In the Governance Report the Joint Standing Committee made wide-ranging recommendations including the following:

- Recommendation 1: That the continuation of self-government for Norfolk Island, as provided for under

the *Norfolk Island Act 1979* (Cth), be conditional on the timely implementation of the specific mechanisms of accountability and reforms to the political system recommended in this report.
- Recommendation 2: That the Federal Government reassess its current policies with respect to Norfolk Island and the basis for the territory's exclusion from Commonwealth programs and services, with a view to determining clearly understood and consistent rationale and framework for Commonwealth funding, advice, and assistance that will be provided across government to the Norfolk Island community.
- Recommendation 9: That the Federal Government review and assess the level of income support and health and medical assistance on Norfolk Island with a view to ensuring parity with entitlements paid to Australian citizens and residents domiciled on the mainland.
- Recommendation 11. That, as recommended by the Human Rights and Equality Opportunity Commission, the Federal Government extend the operation of the *Migration Act 1958* (Cth) in full to the territory of Norfolk Island, and that Schedule 3 of the *Norfolk Island Act 1979* (Cth) be amended to delete reference to "immigration" and to remove from the Norfolk Island Legislative Assembly and administrator their powers with respect to immigration.

In relation to matters dealt with in the electoral report, the recommendations of the committee were as follows:

- Recommendation 1: The committee recommends that

Australian citizenship be reinstated as a requirement for eligibility to vote for and be elected to the Norfolk Island Legislative Assembly, with appropriate safeguards for the right to vote of all those currently on the electoral roll.
- Recommendation 2: The committee recommends that the government amend the appropriate legislation, including the *Norfolk Island Act 1979* and the *Commonwealth Electoral Act 1918*, to ensure that all elections and referenda on Norfolk Island come under the supervision of the Australian Electoral Commission.
- Recommendation 3: The committee recommends that the period for which an Australian citizen must reside on Norfolk Island before being eligible to vote for the legislative assembly be reduced to six months.

Chapter 7

A Measure of Self-Government?

On 3 December 2003 the report of the Commonwealth Parliament's Joint Standing Committee on the National Capital and External Territories inquiry into governance on Norfolk Island was laid before the parliament. The inquiry report was entitled *Quis Custodiet Ipsos Custodes?: Inquiry into Governance on Norfolk Island*. It apparently enjoyed cross-party support in the Federal Parliament, including that of the Coalition, the Australian Labor Party, and the Democrats.

Faced with this onslaught, the Norfolk Island Government pushed back. As well as responding to each of the inquiries listed in chapter 6, the government engaged in three major lobbying efforts to put before the Federal Parliament its point of view. These were the campaign against the Norfolk Island Amendment Bill 1999, the campaign against Minister Jim Lloyd's proposals (including the Bennett High Court litigation), and the campaign against the federal "intervention" which played out over the period of 2006 to 2016. In the first two of those exercises, the government was successful. But not in the third. Each involved professional government relations consultants: Judy Marty in 1999, and Yaron Finkelstein (of Crosby Textor) in respect of Jim Lloyd's proposals.

Lloyd's proposals amounted to an attempt to "roll-back" the degree of autonomy which the island had previously enjoyed. To assist in achieving that end, legal opinions were located or obtained from a number of sources.

A joint opinion by Mr Ellicott and M H McLelland QC dated 11 August 1975 was located, which relevantly concluded that:

- Norfolk Island is, by authority of an imperial Act, "a distinct and separate settlement", and its status as such cannot be altered except by, or pursuant to, an imperial Act. The legislative power conferred on the Commonwealth Parliament by section 122 of the Constitution is restricted to that extent.
- Subject to the above, sovereignty over Norfolk Island is vested in the Crown in right of the Commonwealth of Australia, and the Commonwealth Parliament has power to make laws for the government of Norfolk Island pursuant to section 122 of the Constitution.
- Norfolk Island is, in effect, a Crown Colony of Australia. The Crown in right of the United Kingdom has no surviving powers emanating from section 5 of the 1855 Act [*Australian Waste Lands Act 1855*].

There was also an opinion by Mr McLelland alone, dated 11 August 1975, dealing with Norfolk Island and the United Nations.

There was an opinion of Professor Crawford AC SC FBA dated 9 August 1999 – publicly available by reason of its inclusion in submissions to the Select Committee on the Republic

Referendum – which relevantly concluded that "in my opinion, Norfolk Island is a separate external territory of the Crown in right of the Commonwealth of Australia. Constitutionally, it is not an internal territory and thus not an integral part of the Commonwealth of Australia". Crawford was a professor of law at Cambridge University and latterly a judge of the International Court of Justice.

M H McLelland later became the chief judge in equity in the Supreme Court of New South Wales. A further opinion was, more recently, obtained from Vaughan Lowe KC of the English Bar and Dr Christopher Ward SC of the New South Wales Bar.

From 1 July 2016, a suite of federal Australian legislative measures took effect, including the *Norfolk Island Legislation Amendment Act 2015* (Cth); federal legislation with respect to taxation, social security, biosecurity, customs, immigration, and health arrangements would apply to Norfolk Island from 1 July 2016. A proposed Norfolk Island Regional Council would deal with local government type matters. The *Commonwealth Electoral Act* would also be amended to incorporate Norfolk Island into one of the federal divisions of the Australian Capital Territory and make it compulsory for residents of Norfolk Island to vote in federal elections. These steps follow the adoption in March 2016 of the *Territories Legislation Amendment Act 2016* (Cth) and accompanying *Passenger Movement Charge Amendment (Norfolk Island) Act 2016*. The effect of these measures was to reverse the substantial autonomy which had previously been enjoyed by Norfolk Island.

Dr Ward and Mr Lowe, and to like effect M H McLelland, were asked to advise on the following questions:

a) Is Norfolk Island a non-self-governing territory within the meaning of Article 73 of the Charter of the United Nations?
b) Is United Nations General Assembly Resolution 1514 of 14 December 1960 applicable to Norfolk Island, having regard to the principles expressed in Resolution 1541?
c) What, if any, mechanisms are available to "inscribe" the island under Article 73(e) of the Charter?

Counsel advised as follows:

a) Norfolk Island is a non-self-governing territory within the meaning of Article 73 of the Charter of the United Nations.
b) Yes.
c) By petitioning the Special Committee on the situation with regard to the implementation of the declaration on the granting of independence to colonial countries and peoples ("the Special Committee"), followed by the subsequent approval of the General Assembly, or more directly, by resolution of the General Assembly.

Counsel further observed:

> We wish to emphasise that the ability of a non-self-governing territory to reach a full measure of self-government does not require the territory to become an independent state. Where very small territories are concerned, other forms of relationship such as free association with a state may be more appropriate (as, for example, with the Cook Islands and New Zealand). The crucial point is that the non-self-governing territory has the right to determine its own political status.

In accordance with that advice, a petition accompanied by supporting evidence was submitted.

Vaughan Lowe KC is a London-based barrister operating in the field of international law. Cases in which he has been briefed include *Timor-Leste v. Australia* concerning certain documents (in which he acted as counsel for Timor-Leste).

There has been explicit reliance by senators and members of the Australian Parliament on the proposition that "Norfolk Island is part of the Commonwealth", and this proposition is also repeatedly expressed in both the Governance Report and the Electoral Report. See, for example, the following instances:

- Senate Hansard for December 2003, page 19115, (Senator Hill).
- Senate Hansard for 3 March 2004, page 20635 (Senator O'Brien), page 20638 (Senator Despoja), page 20641 (Senator Lightfoot), page 20644 (Senator Hogg), and page 20647 (Senator Humphries).
- Representatives Hansard 4 March 2004, page 25958 (Mrs Kelly), page 25064 (Mr Thompson), and pages 25969, 25972 (Mr Neville).

Counsel were asked to advise on inter alia the prospects of success in obtaining "curial recognition" of the proposition that Norfolk Island is not a constituent part of the Commonwealth of Australia, but a dependency of the Commonwealth of Australia.

This is not necessarily the same as obtaining a judgement in which, as an essential part of the reasoning, that proposition is affirmed. It might be possible, though it is of course not preferable, for the proposition to be affirmed obiter, even though the proceeding used as a suitable vehicle is itself unsuccessful.

To illustrate the point, if proceedings were taken to dispute the validity of the *Norfolk Island Amendment Act 2004* (as in fact happened), and further, that that Act is held to be a valid exercise of the Federal Parliament's asserted plenary legislative power under section 122 of the Constitution, nevertheless, that outcome would not necessarily preclude a negative answer by the High Court to the following question left open by the joint judgement of Brennan, Deane, and Toohey JJ in *Capital Duplicators Pty Ltd v. The Australian Capital Territory* [1992] 109 ALR 1, 16 namely:

> whether an external colony or territory which was not then [that is, on 1 January 1901] a part of a State can become part of the Commonwealth unless it be admitted into or established by the Commonwealth as a State pursuant to section 121 of the Constitution or is included within the limits of a State pursuant to section 123 of the Constitution.

Hence, it is at least possible that curial recognition of the proposition that Norfolk Island is not part of the Commonwealth might be obtained, even though the particular vehicle (in that case the *Norfolk Island Amendment Act 2004*) is held to be valid.

The point of obtaining such recognition, even if the proceedings constituting a vehicle are themselves unsuccessful, is essentially political. Just as Commonwealth parliamentarians repeatedly assert that Norfolk Island is part of the Commonwealth, and that certain political consequences flow from that fact, curial recognition of the contrary view would enable Norfolk Island authorities to dispute the intellectual underpinning of, for example, many of the recommendations of the Governance Report and also those recommendations of the Electoral Report which have found their way into the *Norfolk Island Amendment Act 2004*.

In this connection, it is to be recalled that the asserted proposition that Norfolk Island is part of the Commonwealth itself derived from arguably obiter passages in the High Court's decision in *Berwick Ltd v. Gray, Deputy Commissioner of Taxation* [1976] 8 ALR 580.

It has been said that a law is authorised by section 122 if it has "sufficient connection or nexus with the good government of the territory" or "a rational connection with the government of the territory". These expressions derive from the judgements of Mason J and Murphy J in *Attorney-General (WA) v. Australian National Airlines Commission*) [1976] 138 CLR 492. They do not directly touch the situation where a law of the parliament is supportable under a head of power in section 51 but the Commonwealth seeks to rely on section 122 in order to avoid a requirement of section 51. In *Australian National Airlines Commission* the law of the parliament under attack was held to be invalid, except in so far as it was a law for the government of the territory under section 122. In *Capital Duplicators v. Australian Capital Territory* [1992] 109 ALR 1 the High Court dealt with the question of whether the Australian Capital Territory Legislative Assembly had power validly to impose a duty of excise, with the meaning of section 90 of the Constitution. The court held that it did not, despite the fact that the "exclusive" power of the Commonwealth Parliament to do so had hitherto been construed as applying so as to exclude only state parliaments (and not territory legislatures) from exercising that power.

If that were all, *Duplicators* would support the proposition that, for example, Norfolk Island customs legislation (before its repeal) was invalid, and by parity of reasoning, that other pre-2015 Norfolk Island legislation dealing with topics that were in conventional constitutional doctrine, the exclusive province of the Federal Parliament, were also invalid.

However, the High Court was careful to avoid any such conclusion, and it did so by drawing a clear distinction between the internal and external territories.

The majority views of the court were expressed in two judgements, a joint judgement of *Brennan, Deane, and Toohey JJ* and a separate judgement of *Gaudron J*.

The joint judgement noted that:

> Section 122 is found in chapter VI of the Constitution – "new States". Section 121, which provides for the admission of new States to the Commonwealth, relates not only to territories which are parts of existing States (sections 123 and 124), but also to such colonies or territories as may be admitted into or established by the Commonwealth as States.

> These latter colonies and territories were not part of the Original States. In the Convention Debates, the forerunner of section 122 was seen primarily, though not necessarily, as designed to provide for the provisional of government of territories as they moved towards statehood.

For the purposes of the decision, the "federal compact" applied only to those territories which initially formed part of the "Original States", that is, the internal territories:

One of the objectives of the federation was the creation of a free trade area embracing the geographical territory of the uniting colonies, that is, the territories of the colonies which became the Original States of the Commonwealth on its establishment on 1 January 1901. The territory of the Commonwealth at that time embraced the whole of the territory of those States, including the Northern Territory of South Australia. *The Commonwealth of Australia Constitution Act ensured that the territory of the Commonwealth was coterminous with the aggregate of the territories of the Original States.* A colony or territory which was not then part of a State did not become part of the Commonwealth. It is unnecessary to consider whether an external colony or territory which was not then a part of a State can become part of the Commonwealth unless it be admitted into or established by the Commonwealth as a state, pursuant to section 121 of the Constitution or is included within the limits of the State, pursuant to section 123 of the Constitution. However, it is clear that the geographical areas which have become mainland Commonwealth territories were parts of States as at 1 January 1901 and are parts of the Commonwealth now.

And to like effect, the remarks in the joint judgement directed to the question of the exclusivity of power secured by section 90 are carefully circumscribed by express reference to "internal territories" – the phrase and its cognates are used five times in the relevant passage.

Gaudron J's judgement includes a cautionary passage relating to Norfolk Island, but the general analysis is on the same footing.

> [The internal territories] and any future Territory brought into existence by separation from one or more of the States are necessarily constituent parts of the Commonwealth of Australia, both geographically and politically. Other territory might become part of Australia if, for example, the limits of a State are increased to include it, and some territory may be part of the Commonwealth even though it was not in 1901 and is not now within the limits of any state (see, with respect to Norfolk Island, *Berwick v. Gray* (1976) 133 CLR 603, per Mason J at 608). But, as is apparent from the external territories which were held under mandate from the League of Nations and, later, under trusteeship from the United Nations, *the mere acquisition of territory does not, of itself, make that territory a constituent part of the Commonwealth either in a political or geographical sense.*

And the nature of the federal compact (to which the Norfolk Island people were not party), is of significance in this context, as Gaudron J explains:

> The agreement recited in the preamble to the Constitution, namely to "unite in one indissoluble Federal Commonwealth" may well require that some distinction be made for

the purposes of section 122 between territory which, geographically and politically, is a constituent part of the Commonwealth and territory which is not.

Her Honour again emphasised the desirability of minimising "disjunction", while expressly confining that trend to the internal territories, in her 1994 minority judgement in *Svikart v. Stewart* [1994] 125 ALR 534:

> Although there are differences between a territory and a State and, although the power to legislate for the government of a territory conferred by section 122 of the Constitution is different from the power to legislate with respect to identified topics conferred by section 51, the *internal* territories are part of the Commonwealth of Australia and the Australian resident in those territories are part of its body politic.

See also *Teori Tan v. Commonwealth* [1969] HCA 62 on which date the question was squarely addressed. However, more recently the line of cases in which Teori Tau was influential was overruled in a recent case cited as *Commonwealth v. Yunupingu* [2025] HCA 6.

It seems to be recognised that the question of Norfolk Island's status remains open. In argument before the court in *Attorney-General (Commonwealth) v. Tse* on 5 March 1998 (the actual decision is irrelevant for present purposes), the following exchange occurred:

> *Mr Jackson* [Counsel]: Well, your Honour has a lot of territories of a disparate kind in relation to which not even

the members of the Court agree sometimes about whether, for example, the mainland Territories of Australia, ACT, Jervis Bay Territory, and the Northern Territory, are or are not part of the Commonwealth. Sorry, I should put it the other way around: they are part of the Commonwealth, but whether other territories are or are not seems to be a matter of dispute. *Capital Duplicators (No. 1)*, I think, was the case where your Honour Justice Gaudron dealt with that some . . .

Gaudron J: I think there is some dispute as to whether they are part of the Commonwealth anyway, still.

Mr Jackson: Yes.

McHugh J: There certainly is.

Mr Jackson: The dicta in *Berwick Limited v. Gray* do not seem to have commanded universal acceptance since then.

All of which seems to the writer to be consistent with the notion that the question of whether Norfolk Island is or is not a "part of" metropolitan Australia is a live issue which might be capable of determination by the High Court in due course.

However, the focus of attention has now passed to whether Norfolk Island is or is not a non-self-governing territory within the meaning of the UN Charter. It seems plainly indicated by eminent counsel that the answer to that question is more readily capable of determination than speculative proceedings in domestic tribunals.

Further straws in the wind are the "additional comments" of Senators Pocock and McLachlan to the JSCNCET, as follows:

- "Norfolk Island is a distinct and separate territory and entitled to determine its own future in accordance with the aspirations of its people (Senator McLachlan)."
- "The people of Norfolk Island are a distinct and separate community with very different needs and aspirations to those of the Australian community (Senator Pocock)."

SELECT BIBLIOGRAPHY

Barrow, John, *Eventful history of the Bounty: A Description of Pitcairn's Island*, Harper & Bros., New York, 1839.

British Government, *Correspondence relating to the Transfer of Norfolk Island to the Government of New South Wales*, Presented to Parliament by Command of Her Majesty, February 1897, Eyre & Spottiswoode, London, 1897.

British Parliamentary Papers, 'Removal of inhabitants of Pitcairn's Island to Norfolk Island' in *Colonies: Australia, 1857*, Vol. 22, 1857, Irish University Press, Shannon, Ireland, 1969.

British Parliamentary Papers, 'Pitcairn Islanders (Norfolk Island)' in *Colonies: Australia, 1862-1863*, Vol. 24, Irish University Press, Shannon Island, 1969, p.1.

British Parliament, *Correspondence relating to the Transfer of Norfolk Island to the Government of New South Wales*, Her Majesty's Stationery Office, London, February 1897, ML Q991.9/5A1.

Brock, W. R., *Britain and the Dominions*, Cambridge University Press, Cambridge, 1951.

Brodie, G. E., Report No. 17, Vol. 1, *Votes & Proceedings*, New South Wales Legislative Assembly, 15 December 1898.

Brodie, Walter, *Pitcairn's Island and the Islanders*, Whittaker & Co., London, 1851.

Clark, C. M. H., *A History of Australia*, Vol. 1, Melbourne University Press, Carlton, Vic., 1985.

Colonial Office, London, 'Governor's commission and

instructions, 24 June 1856', *Laws and regulations of Norfolk Island*, NAA AA/1970/374/1.

Commonwealth Government of Australia, *Opinions of the Attorneys-General of the Commonwealth of Australia*, Vol. 1, 1901-1914, AGPS, Canberra, 1981.

Duke, J. S., Mary-Lorraine Duke, Angela Guymer, Merval Hoare, Nan Smith, *Norfolk Island Hospitals and Public Health from the 1st Convict Settlement*, Norfolk Island Historical Society, Norfolk Island, 1994.

Dyster, Barrie and David Meredith, *Australia in the international economy in the twentieth century*, Cambridge University Press, Cambridge, U.K., 1991.

Gillespie, Oliver A., *The Pacific: Official History of New Zealand in World War II, 1939-1945*, War History Branch, Department of Internal Affairs, Wellington, New Zealand, 1952.

Hampden, Governor Viscount, *Correspondence relating to the Transfer of Norfolk Island to the Government of New South Wales*, presented to Parliament by Command of Her Majesty, February 1897, Her Majesty's Stationery Office, London, 1897.

Hitch, G, *The Pacific War 1941-1945 and Norfolk Island*, Norfolk Island, 1992 (reprinted in 1996).

Hoare, Merval, *Norfolk Island: a history through illustration, 1774-1974*, AGPS, Canberra, 1979.

Hoare, Merval, *Norfolk Island: 1774-1998*, Central Queensland University Press, Rockhampton, 1999.

Hoare, Merval, *The Winds of Change: Norfolk Island 1950-1982*, University of South Pacific, Suva, Fiji, 1983.

Hoare, *Norfolk Island*, University of Queensland Press (4th edition), 1988.

Hunt, Atlee, Secretary Department of External Affairs, *Memorandum relating to Norfolk Island*, 13 November 1914.

Immerwahr, Daniel, *How to hide an empire – a short history of the Greater United States*, Random House, 2019.

Jervis, James, 'The Pitcairn Islanders' in *R.A.H.S. Journal & Proceedings*, Vol. 22, 1936, p. 376; Vol. 25, 1939, pp. 331-337.

Kerr, A. *A Federation in the Seas*, Attorney-General's Department, 2009.

London Missionary Society, *Narrative of the Mission at Otaheite and other islands in the South Seas, commenced by London Missionary Society in year 1797*, London Missionary Society, London, 1818.

McIntyre Stuart, *The Oxford History of Australia*, Vol. 4, 1901-1942, Oxford Dictionary Press, Melbourne, 1990.

Murray, T. B., *Pitcairn: the Island, the People and the Pastor*, Society for Promoting Christian Knowledge, London, Haskell House Publishers Ltd, Publishers of Scarce Scholarly Books, New York, 1972.

New South Wales Parliament, Legislative Assembly Debates.

New South Wales Parliament, Legislative Council Debates.

Nicholson, R. B. *The Pitcairners*, Angus & Robertson, Sydney, 1965.

Nobbs, Chris, *Australia's Assault on Norfolk Island 2017-18*, Norfolk Island, 2019.

Nobbs, Chris, *Australia's Assasult on Norfolk Island 2019-20*, Norfolk Island, 2021.

Nobbs Raymond, *George Hunn Nobbs, 1799-1884*, The Pitcairn Descendants Society of Norfolk Island, 1984.

Nobbs, Raymond, ed., *Norfolk Island and its First Settlement, 1788-1814*, Library of Australian History, North Sydney, 1988.

Nobbs, Raymond, ed., *Norfolk Island and its Second Settlement, 1825-1855*, Library of Australian History, Sydney, 1991.

Norfolk Island Advisory Council Minutes, 1935-1960.

Norfolk Island Council Minutes, 1960-1961.

Norfolk Island Executive Council Minutes, 1921-1935.

O'Collins, Maev, *An Uneasy Relationship, Norfolk Island and the Commonwealth of Australia*, Pandanus Books, Research School of Pacific and Asian Studies, A.N.U., Canberra, A.C.T., 2002.

Oliver, Alexander, Commissioner, *Report on Norfolk Island, (Supplementary)*, 14 March 1904, NAA CP697/99/1, Item 1, 1904; *Evidence of Oliver report* (typescript), SR.,7/4121.

Royal Commission on Norfolk Island Affairs, (F. Whysall, Commissioner), *Report*, Government Printer, Victoria, 12 August 1926.

Stanley Gibbons Stamp Catalogue, Part 1, British Commonwealth 1988, ninetieth edition, Stanley Gibbons Publications Ltd., London and Ringwood, 1987.

Treadgold, M. L., *Bounteous Bestowal: the economic history of Norfolk Island*, Pacific Research Monograph No. 18, A.N.U. Canberra, 1988.

Waldegrove, W., 'Extracts from Journal of H.M.S. Seringpatam in the Pacific, 1830', in *Royal Geographical Society of London Journal*, Vol. 3, pp. 156-168.

Ward, Russel, *A Nation for a Continent: the history of Australia 1901-1975*, Heinemann Educational Australia, Richmond, Victoria, 1983.

Waterlow and Sons Limited, Printers, *Via Pacific: Some Notes on the Pacific Cable*, London Wall, London, 1912.

Wilkinson, Henry, *Papers relating to Colonial Possessions*, London, 1885-1886; SRL, DS339.206/7.

Wright, Donald R., The Constitutional Status of Norfolk Island in Domestic Law, 15 March 1999, paras. 18-19.

Wright, Donald R., *Paper to Norfolk Island Government about previous proposals relating to workers' compensation*, 22 August 1984, Administration File (Old Series) 1/1/73.

Newspapers and Journals

Chambers's Edinburgh Journal, 'The Pitcairn Islanders in 1849', pp 10-12 (ML Mss. F999.7/P).

Daily Telegraph.

Norfolk Island Weekly.

Sydney Morning Herald.

The Illustrated London News, 'Jubilee Sermon' of Society for Promoting Christian Knowledge, Vol. 14, 10 March 1849, p. 157.

The Mirror, 'Spirit of Discovery', 1831, p. 375 (ML Mss F999.7/P).

Libraries and Archives

Mitchell Library, Sydney.

National Archives of Australia, Canberra.

Public Record Office, London.

State Library of New South Wales, Sydney.

State Records of New South Wales, Sydney and Kingswood

ABBREVIATIONS

AC	Advisory Council, Norfolk Island
AGPS	Australian Government Publishing Service
AR	Annual Report, Norfolk Island
BPP	British Parliamentary Papers
CO	Colonial Office, London
DT	*Daily Telegraph*
E.C.	Executive Council, Norfolk Island
LAPD	Legislative Assembly Parliamentary Debates
LMS	London Missionary Society
ML	Mitchell Library, Sydney
NAA	National Archives of Australia, Canberra, A.C.T.
PRO	Public Record Office, London
RAHS	Royal Australian Historical Society
R.G.S.L.J.	Royal Geographic Society of London, Journal
SMH	*Sydney Morning Herald*
SPCK	Society for Promoting Christian Knowledge
SR	State Records, Sydney
SRL	State Reference Library, State Library of New South Wales, Sydney

END NOTES

CHAPTER 1: ANNIE AND THE EMPIRE

1. For collected papers relating to this case, see Peden Family Collection, ML MSS 1663.29. Sir John Beverley Peden, who died in 1946, was Dean of the Faculty of Law in the University of Sydney, and President of the Legislative Council of New South Wales, The papers include a printed pamphlet marked "Strictly Confidential". "The Administration of Justice in Norfolk Island, and the case of Annie Charlotte Greena Wiseman Christian. 1893": Sydney, Charles Potter, Government Printer, 1894 (hereafter "Peden Collection" or "PC"). All quoted passages relating to this case are taken from the Peden Collection, unless otherwise indicated.

2. Despatch Norfolk Island No 6, 2 December 1893, Governor of NSW [Duff] to Colonial Secretary, ML.

3. Despatch CO 201/614, 2 February 1893, Governor of NSW [Jersey] to Colonial Secretary ML.

4. Despatch CO 201/509, 22 January 1859, Governor of NSW [Denison] to Colonial Secretary. ML.

5. Despatch Norfolk Island No. 5, 2 December 1893, Governor of NSW [Duff] to Colonial Secretary. ML (Peden Collection).

6. Governor of NSW [Duff] to (Colonial) Attorney-General,

24 October 1893. Enclosure in Despatch Norfolk Island No 5: note 5, supra.

7. Barton to Governor of Norfolk Island, 21 November 1893. ML (Peden Collection).

8. Governor of New South Wales to Marquis of Ripon, Despatch Norfolk Island No 7, 4 June 1894, CO 201/615.

9. Governor R W Duff to Secretary of State for Colonies, Despatch Norfolk Island No. 5, 2 December 1893, PC.

10. Private letter from Mr Meade to Sir R Duff, 17 January 1894, PC.

11. Despatch Norfolk Island No. 7, note 8 supra.

12. Despatch Norfolk Island No 7, note 8 supra.

13. Docker's Report to Private Secretary, Governor of New South Wales, 22 June 1894, PC. Transmitted to Colonial Office 15 October 1894, Despatch No. 11.

14. 29 and 30 November 1894, to Mr Bramston. PC.

15. British Parliamentary Papers, *Correspondence Relating to the Transfer of Norfolk Island to the Government of New South Wales*, London, HMSO, 1897 (hereafter "CRT"), page 3.

16. CRT, page 3.

17. CRT, page 4.

18. CRT, page 5.

19. CRT, page 5.

20. CRT, pages 7-8. Emphasis supplied.

21. CRT, page 8.

22. CRT, page 14.

23. CRT, page 16.

24. CRT, page 12.

25. CRT, page 21.

26. CRT, page 25.

27. CRT, page 26.

28. Emphasis supplied.

29. Emphasis supplied.

30. Emphasis supplied.

31. Minister for External Affairs (Mr Glynn) House of Representatives, *Hansard*, 16 September 1913, 1241.

32. O'Connell and Riordan, *Opinions on Imperial Constitutional Law*, LBC 1971, pages 306-308.

33. *Norfolk Island – Constitutional and Legal Status*, joint opinion by R J Ellicott QC and M. H. McLelland QC, 11 August 1975, author's collection.

34. *Opinions of the Attorneys-General of the Commonwealth of Australia*, Volume 1, 1901-14, AGPS, Canberra, 1981, pages 267-268.

CHAPTER 2: PITCAIRN ISLAND

1. R. B. Nicolson, *The Pitcairners*, Angus & Robertson, printed by Halstead Press, Sydney, 1965, pp.xiv, 33.

2. Donald McLoughlin, *Law and Order on Pitcairn's Island*, Commissioner for Pitcairn Island, Auckland, 2000.

3. Thomas B. Murray, *Pitcairn: the Island, the People and the Pastor*, first published 1860 by Society for Promoting Christian Knowledge, London, Haskell House Publishers Ltd, New York, 1972, pp. 69-83.

4. R. B. Nicolson, pp. 15, 18, 25-27, 34-35; C. H. Currey, 'An Outline of the Story of Norfolk Island and Pitcairn's Island, 1788-1857' in Royal Australian Historical Society, *Journal & Proceedings*, Vol. 44, 1958, pp. 328-330.

5. C. H. Currey, pp. 338-340.

6. R. B. Nicolson, p. 58.

7. Walter Brodie, *Pitcairn's Island and the Islanders*, Whittaker & Co., London, 1851, p. 83; R.B. Morris & G. W. Irwin, *An Encyclopaedia of the Modern World*, Weidensfield & Nicolson, London 1970, p. 352; *The Cambridge History of the British Empire*, 1783-1870, Vol. 2, Cambridge University Press, Cambridge, 1940, p. 280; W.R. Brock, *Britain and the Dominions*, Cambridge University Press, Cambridge, 1951, pp. 69-70, C. H. Currey, p. 356.

8. *Encyclopaedia Britannica*, Vol. 10, William Benton, U.S.A., 1961, p. 709.

9. Richard M. Brace, *The Making of the Modern World*, Second Edition – Enlarged, Holt, Rinehart & Winston, Inc., New York, 1961, pp. 346-351; Stuart McIntyre, 'Liberalism', in Graeme Davison, John Hirst, Stuart McIntyre (eds), in *The Oxford Companion to Australian History*, Oxford University Press, Melbourne, 1998, p. 388.

10. London Missionary Society, *History of the establishment and progress of the Christian religion in the Islands of the South Sea*, Tappan & Dennet, Boston, 1841, pp. 62, 109-110.

11. London Missionary Society, *Narrative of the Mission at Otaheite and other islands in the South Seas, commenced by London Missionary Society in year 1797*, L.M.S. London, 1818, pp. 6-9.

12. John Barrow, *Eventful History of the Bounty: A Description of Pitcairn's Island*, Harper & Bros., New York, 1839, p. 347, W. Brodie, p. 82.

13. *Sydney Gazette*, 17 July 1819, p. 3.

14. John Barrow, 'Recent Accounts of the Pitcairn Islanders, extracts from private journals of Captain W. Waldegrove and Captain A. A. Sandilands' read 10 June 1833 in *Royal Geographical Society of London, Journal*, Vol. 3, 1833, page 159.

15. Raymond Nobbs, *George Hunn Nobbs, 1799-1884, Chaplain of Pitcairn and Norfolk Island*, The Pitcairn Descendants Society, Norfolk Island, 1984, pp. 2, 5-13; Charles Lucas (ed.), *The Pitcairn Island Register Book*, Society for Promoting Christian Knowledge, London, 1929, pp. 6, 12, Donald McLoughlin, p. 14; A.S.C. Ross & A. W. Moverley, with contributions by Alaric Maude and ors. *The Pitcairnese Language*, Andre Deutsch, 1964, p. 66.

16. Captain Fremantle, R. N., in John Barrow, 'Recent Accounts...', p. 164; Charles Lucas, pp. 16-17; C. H. Currey, p. 345; A. S. C. Ross & A. W. Moverley, p. 67.

17. Charles Lucas, pp. 18-19.

18. R. B. Nicolson, p. 135.

19. D. McLoughlin, pp. 21-22

20. R. B. Nicolson, pp. 135-139.

21. J. T. Salmon, *Native Trees of New Zealand*, A. H. & A. W. Reed Limited, Wellington, New Zealand, 1980, p. 59.

22. Quoted in Walter Brodie, pp. 82-91.

23. ibid., p. 92.

24. ibid., pp. 91-106.

25. Burroughs Wellcombe & Co., *Crown and Realm: Souvenir of the Coronation of King George V*, London, 1911, pp. 165-274.

26. D. McLoughlin, p. 14; C. Lucas, p. 1; R. B. Nicolson, app. 1; other Register entries in T. B. Murray, pp. 259-361; and W. Brodie, pp. 107-249.

27. *Register*, cited in W. Brodie, pp. 117-153.

28. F. M. Bladen, pp. 2-3.

29. W. Brodie, pp. 79, 250.

30. ibid., pp. 79-80.

31. C. H. Currey, pp. 357-9, T. B. Murray, pp. 218-220.

32. C. H. Currey, p. 359; T. B. Murray, p. 232.

33. C. H. Currey, p. 359.

34. British Parliamentary Papers, Colonies: Australia, *Correspondence on the subject of Removal of Inhabitants of Pitcairn's Island to Norfolk Island*, Vol. 22, 1857, Irish University Press, Shannon Island, 1969, p. 26.

35. C. H. Currey, pp. 360-361.

36. Merval Hoare, *Norfolk Island: A history through illustration, 1774-1974*, p. 52; BPP, 1857, p. 25.

37. C. H. Currey, p. 357; BPP, 1857, p. 25.

38. T. B. Murray, p. 362.

39. F. M. Bladen, p. 8; C. H. Currey, pp. 363, 367; T. B. Murray, pp. 362, 369, 378.

CHAPTER 3: NORFOLK ISLAND

1. The journals of Captain James Cook on his Voyages of Discovery, Volume 2, Hakluyt Society, Extra Series No XXXV. Pages 565-568.

2. Phillip's First Commission 1786 Historical Records of Australia, Series 1 (the Library Committee of the Commonwealth Parliament, 1914), page 1.

3. 1787: Act 27 GeoIII cap2.

4. 1795: Act 34 GeoIII cap45.

5. 1831: Governor Bourke's commission 25 June 1831; Historical Records of Australia, Series 1, Vol 16 (A Library Committee of the Commonwealth Parliament), 1914, page 837.

6. Order in Council 29 September 1843 under Act 6&7 Vict cap 35.

7. Extract from *Mabo & Ors v Queensland (No 2)* (1992) 175 CLR 1.

8. Royal Instructions issued under Imperial Order in Council of 24 June 1856.

9. Extract from Sir William Denison, *Varieties of Vice-Regal Life*, Longman Green & Co, London, 1870, Vol 1 (hereafter VVRL), page 411.

10. VVRL, pages 412-413.

11. VVRL, page 413.

12. VVRL, pages 425-426.

13. *Journal and Proceedings of the Australian Historical Society*, 1906, Vol II, Part 1, page 11.

14. *The Norfolk Island Pioneer* (newspaper), Vol 1, No XX11, 1 November 1886 (hereafter "NIP"), page 1.

15. NIP, page 2.

16. NIP, page 2.

17. Peden Family Collection, ML, MSS 1663.29. See above.

CHAPTER 4: HOPE AND DISAPPOINTMENT 1914-1939

1. M L Treadgold, *Bounteous Bestowal: The Economic History of Norfolk Island*, Pacific Research Monograph No 18, ANU, Canberra, 1988, p. 127.

2. B Dyster & D Meredith, *Australia in the International Economy in the 20th Century*, Cambridge University Press, Cambridge, UK, 1991, pp 49, 51.

3. S McIntyre, ibid, Item 4, pp 142-143.

4. S McIntyre, pp 145-6.

5. Maev O'Collins, *Uneasy Relationship, Norfolk Island and the Commonwealth of Australia*. Pananas Books, Research School of Pacific and Asian Studies, ANU, Canberra, ACT, 2002, p. 102; AR 1929, p.10.

6. ibid, pp 87-93.

End Notes

7. Australia, House of Representatives, Debates, 2 June 1915, pp 3617-3620.

8. ibid, pp 10 June 1915, pp 3920-3921, Maev O'Collins, p. 61.

9. ibid, 10 June 1915, p. 3923.

10. AR, 1915, pp 3-6.

11. AR, 1918, p. 7.

12. AR, 1926

13. Whysall, p. 55.

14. F Whysall, Commissioner, Royal Commission on Norfolk Island Affairs, Report, Government Printer, Victoria, 12 August 1926, p. 55.

15. AR, 1925, pp 7-8.

16. F Whysall, pp 10-11.

17. ibid, pp 9-11, 55.

18. ibid, pp 14-15.

19. Executive Council Minutes, 14 May 1926.

20. F Whysall, pp 21-22, EC Minutes, 14 May 1926.

21. EC Minutes, 3 June 1926.

22. F Whysall, pp. 20-22.

23. ibid, pp 15-20.

24. ibid, pp 43-44.

25. ibid, pp 55-57.

26. M O Collins, p. 121.
27. AR, 1926, p. 1.
28. AR, 1930, p. 10.
29. AR, 1931, p. 4.
30. AR, 1932, p. 10; ..... p. 127.
31. AR, 1933, p. 11.
32. AR, 1934, p. 12.
33. AC Minutes, 4 January 1934, p. 2, verbatim, 19 May 1934, pp 1-2.
34. Prime Minister's minutes, 14 December 1934, 14 January 1935, NAA A5118, A/800/1-4 Part 1.
35. ibid, 14 January 1935, Prime Minister's minutes re deportation of JA MacArthur-Onslow, 9 January 1935, NAA A518, 0/800/411/4.
36. ibid.
37. EC Minutes, 28 and 30 March 1935.
38. ibid, 30 March 1935.
39. F Whysall, p 21.
40. AR, 1936-1937 NP.
41. EC Minutes, 1 May, 5 June 1935.
42. ibid, 26 July 1935.
43. AC Minutes, 27 November 1936, 8 November 1936.
44. AR, 1936, 1937.

CHAPTER 5: WORLD WAR II AND POST-WAR RECONSTRUCTION: 1940-1965

1. R. Ward, *A Nation for a Continent: the history of Australia 1901-1975*, Heinemann Educational Australia, Richmond, Victoria, 1983, p. 187.

2. ibid., pp 234-237, S McIntyre, p. 326.

3. ibid., p. 247.

4. Oliver A. Gillespie, *The Pacific: Official History of Ne Zealand in World War II, 1939-1945*, War History Branch, Department of Internal Affairs, Wellington, New Zealand, 1952, pp 57-60.

5. S McIntyre, p. 326.

6. Major-General Charles Rosenthal, Administrator, to Prime Minister, 15 September 1939, NAA A518, A16/2/4, 1938-1939.

7. *AR* 1939-1940, p. 1.

8. *AR* 1940-1941, p. 3.

9. A Gillespie, pp 300-301; M L Treadgold, p. 163.

10. R J Rain, Surveyor-General and Chief Property Officer, to Department of Interior, Works & Services Branch, Sydney, 27 November 1941, NAA Sydney, SP857/10/0, PR/434, Box 1123, 1941-1962.

11. *AR* 1942-1944, p. 2.

12. M I Treadgold, p 170, *AR* 1942-1944, p. 2.

13. A Gillespie, pp 300-305; M L Treadgold, p 168.

14. M L Treadgold, p. 164.

15. *AR* 1944-1945, p. 3.

16. F Whysall, pp 12-13.

17. Islanders' petition to Governor-General, 31 July 1934, NAA A518, A800/1/4, Part 1.

18. ibid., 3 April 1935.

19. Visit of Sir George Pearce, Minister in Charge of Territories and Norfolk Island Association, 1934-1935, Report, 4 April 1935, NAA A518, A800/1/4, Part 1.

20. Advisory Council Minutes, 1 May 1936, pp 3-5.

21. M L Treadgold, p. 165.

22. ibid, p. 178.

23. ibid.

24. G J Butland, *Report to Department of the Capital Territory of the Australian Government on long term population study of Norfolk Island*, University of New England, Armidale, 31 March 1974, quoted in M L Treadgold, p. 179.

25. ibid., p. 169.

26. ibid., p. 178-181.

27. *Norfolk Island Weekly*, 8 February, 7 March 1941.

28. Advisory Council Minutes, 25 November 1935.

29. Advisory Council Minutes, 24 December 1941, 1 and 25 July 1942, 5 January 1943.

30. Department of External Affairs Minute, 8 June 1943, NAA A518/1, H800/1/4, Part 8, 1943-1945.

31. ibid., pp 2-3, Advisory Council Minutes, 22 January 1943.

32. ibid.

33. Charles Rosenthal to Department of External Territories, 15 December 1943, attached Advisory Council Minutes, 10 December 1943.

34. Advisory Council Minute, 22 January 1943; *Printers and Newspapers Ordinance*, 1935-1936, 8 May 1964, NAA A518, A846/3/54.

35. *Stanley Gibbons Stamp Catalogue*, Part 1, British Commonwealth 1988, ninetieth edition, Stanley Gibbons Publications Ltd., London and Ringwood, 1987, p. 632.

36. Augustus Loftus to CO, 5 March 1885, in Henry Wilkinson, *Papers relating ...* , pp 279-280.

37. *AR* 1948, p. 8.

38. Merval Hoare, 1999, p. 115.

39. *AR* 1949, p. 12.

40. Atlee Hunt, *Memorandum relating ...* , March 1914, p. 29.

41. *AR* 1928, p. 10.

42. *AR* 1930, p. 10.

43. Melanesian Mission to Home & Territories Department, 27 February 1929; Norfolk Island Hospital Board to Prime Minister, 1 May 1929, NAA A518/1, D614/1, Part 1; *AR* 1930, p.10.

44. *AR* 1938-1939, p. 12.

45. *AR* 1947, p. 10; *AR* 1948, p. 9.

46. *AR* 1949, p. 6.

47. Advisory Council Minutes, 3 June 1953, p. 2.

48. John S Duke, Mary-Lorraine Duke, Angela Guymer, Merval Hoare, Nan Smith, *Norfolk Island Hospitals and Public Health from the 1st Convict Settlement*, Norfolk Island Historical Society, Norfolk Island, 1994, pp 32-35.

49. Norfolk Island Progress Association, 9 August 1954, NAA A518, EX618/3.

50. ibid.

51. ibid.; Advisory Council Minutes, 25 March 1955.

52. Advisory Council Minutes, 4 May 1955.

53. Norfolk Island Progress Association to South Pacific Commission, 15 June 1955, NAA 518/1, AO800/1/4.

54. *The Christian Science Monitor*, 28 March 1955; *Pacific Islands Monthly*, August 1960.

55. Advisory Council Minutes, 5 October 1955, p. 4.

56. ibid., 2 May 1956.

57. Norfolk Island Progress Association, 17 September 1956, NAA A518/1, EX618/3

58. ibid., 27 March 1957.

59. Advisory Council Minutes, 1 May 1957, 5 March 1958, 2 April 1958.

60. AR 1958-1959, pp 6-7; *Norfolk Island Act* 1957.

61. Paul Hasluck, *Norfolk News*, 29 October 1959.

62. Merval Hoare, *The Winds of Change: Norfolk Island 1950-1982*, University of South Pacific, Suva, Fiji, 1983, pp 14-20.

63. *Policy of administration of Norfolk Island Council*, NAA A452, 60/4807, 5 July 1960.
64. ibid., 25 August 1960.
65. Government of Norfolk Island, *Constitutional Authority*, NAA A452/1, 1961/1226, 10 January 1961.
66. *Policy of administration ...* , 24 March 1961.
67. ibid., 24 March, 7 April 1961.
68. ibid., 7-8 April 1961.
69. ibid., 26 April 1961.
70. ibid., 7 July 1961.
71. Norfolk Island Council Minutes of Special Meeting, 10 August 1961, NAA A452/1, 1961/5533, p. 8.
72. ibid., pp 8, 15.
73. *Policy of administration ...* , 5 September 1962.
74. ibid., 20 September 1962.
75. *Norfolk News*, 7, 14 November 1963.
76. ibid., 14 May 1964.
77. Advisory Council Minutes, 13 September 1936.
78. ibid., 8 November 1950.
79. ibid.
80. *The Norfolk Island Times*, 19 April, 8 May 1935.

CHAPTER 6: NIMMO AND AFTER

1. Report of the Royal Commission into matters relating to Norfolk Island, AGPS, October 1976 ("Nimmo").
2. Nimmo, p. 5.
3. Nimmo, pp 6-8.
4. Nimmo, p 10.
5. Nimmo, p 12.
6. Nimmo, p. 12.
7. Nimmo, p. 15.
8. Nimmo, p 18.
9. Minutes of Conference at Norfolk Island, 2.15pm, 7 June 1977, author's collection.
10. Norfolk Island Council views on the Nimmo report.
11. Introduction to a statement of the views of the Norfolk Island Council on the Nimmo report, p. 3.
12. *The Norfolk Island News*/March-April 1979, p. 5.
13. Minutes of meeting of the Norfolk Island Council and the Minister of Home Affairs, Martin Place, Sydney, 26 March 1979.
14. *Berwick Ltd v Gray, Deputy Commissioner of Taxation*, (1976) 8 ALR 580.
15. Media release, 8 May 1978.
16. Minutes of meeting, 26 March 1979.
17. ibid.

ACKNOWLEDGEMENTS

I wish to thank **Jessica Mudditt** and **Sinead Heap** for their expert editorial guidance and support while this book was in the press.

I also thank Carolyn Simpson, an expert in rendering an author's attempts at clarity.

The majority of the technical work on this book was undertaken by **Marsha Lake** and I am most grateful to her for her endeavours.

This book came about by courtesy of Geoff Bennett. Without his support and encouragement it would never have been finished. I thank him most sincerely.

INDEX

Symbols

18 and 19 Vict c.54, s.46, 79
1897 Order, 25, 26, 27, 78
1897 Order in Council, 25, 78
1900 Order, 26

A

ABDA area, 145
ABDA Command, 146
Account of a Voyage Around the World, 34
A C Palmer, 105
Act 18 and 19 Vict, c.56, s.5 73
Administration Law 1913, 113, 136
Administration Ordinance, 1935 136
Administrator Alex Wilson, 203
Administrator H B Norman, 176
Administrator J W Parnell, 108
Admiral Chester Nimitz, 147
Admiral Moresby, 58, 61
Admiral Ross, 54
Admiral Thomas C Hart, 145
Advisory Council, 133, 134, 164, 166, 168, 178, 186, 251, 254, 266, 267, 268, 269
Advisory Council Ordinance, 134, 164
Advisory Council Ordinance, 1935, 134
Air squadrons, 144
A J McGrath, 162
Alexander Smith, 36
Allies, 144, 145, 152

Amending Appeals Ordinance, 114
America, 34, 38, 145, 185
Annie, 3, 6, 7, 8, 9, 10, 14, 16, 77, 255
Annie Charlotte Greena Wiseman Christian, 6, 255
Anson Bay, 161
Anzac area, 146
Anzac Naval Force, 146
Arthur Quintal, *Jun*, 58, 68
Article 73, 224, 239
Article 73(e) of the Charter, 239
Article 73 of the Charter of the United Nations, 239
Article 73 of the UN Charter, 224
A S Bathie, 191
A S Gazzard, 161
Atlee Hunt, 99, 105, 171, 267
Attorney-General (Commonwealth) v. Tse, 246
Attorney-General (WA) v. Australian National Airlines Commission) [1976] 138 CLR 492, 242
Auckland, 125, 147, 152, 170, 173, 257
Australia, 2, 4, 26, 27, 29, 34, 79, 80, 81, 82, 85, 88, 95, 96, 98, 99, 100, 101, 102, 105, 106, 107, 108, 110, 111, 118, 119, 123, 129, 137, 141, 142, 144, 145, 146, 147, 149, 156, 161, 169, 170, 171, 175, 181, 182, 198, 209, 210, 216, 217, 218, 219, 221, 225, 232, 233, 237, 238, 240, 244, 245, 246, 247, 249, 250, 251, 252, 253, 254, 257, 260, 261, 262, 263, 265
Australian Capital Territory, 158, 211, 215, 238, 241, 242
Australian Comforts Fund, 149
Australian Department of Main Roads, 150
Australian Electoral Commission, 235
Australian Imperial Force, 101
Australian Parliament, 221, 240
Australian Red Cross, 149
Australian Territories, 217
Australian Waste Lands Act 1855, 24, 27, 30, 31, 60, 65, 85, 92, 237
Australian Waste Lands Act 1855 (18 & 19 Vic c56), section 5, 30

B

Bailey, 179, 191, 198, 199
Ball Bay, 138
Batavia, 39
Belgium, 100, 101
Bennett, 122, 123, 124, 223, 236, 271
Bennett High Court litigation, 236
Berwick case, section 14 of the Norfolk Island Act 1957–1963, 217
Berwick Ltd v. Gray, Deputy Commissioner of Taxation [1976] 8 ALR 580, 242
Bishop's house, 173
Blucher, 223
Boarding Houses Ordinance 1955, 205
Borob, 50
Bounty, 4, 11, 18, 35, 36, 37, 40, 249, 259
Bounty Bay, 36
Brennan, Deane, and Toohey JJ, 241, 243
Brigadier H B Norman, 205
Britain, 38, 39, 40, 43, 46, 56, 99, 100, 101, 144, 145, 148, 249, 258
British Consul at Raiatea, 58
British Crown, 40, 81
British Navy, 44, 56
British sphere, 146
Browns Water, 35
B Toup Nicolas, 58, 116
Buffett, 43, 44, 46, 55, 58, 223
Burma, 145, 146

C

Calcutta, 43
Calcutta Committee, 43
Callao, 54
Cambridge University, 238, 249, 250, 258, 262
Canada, 9, 144

Capital Duplicators Pty Ltd v. The Australian Capital Territory [1992] 109 ALR 1, 241
Capital Duplicators v. Australian Capital Territory [1992] 109 ALR 1, 242
Captain AA Sandilands, 45
Captain Arthur Phillip, 63
Captain Charles R Pinney, 124
Captain Edward Edwards, 35
Captain Fanshawe, 56
Captain Fremantle, 45, 59, 259
Captain Hall, 43
Captain Henry Hunt, 55
Captain H J Worth, 55
Captain H M Denham, 62
Captain James Cook, 63, 261
Captain James Henderson, 43
Captain James Wilson, 42
Captain Jenkin Jones, 54
Captain J Shepherd, 54
Captain Mayhew Folger, 37
Captain Philip Carteret, 34
Captain Pinney, 139
Captain Pipon, 37
Captain Russell Elliot, 68
Captain Russell Elliott, 38
Captain Thompson, 54
Captain T Wood, 55
Captain William Bligh, 35
Captain Woodbridge, 55
Captain Worth, 61
Captain W P Hitchcock, 151
Cascade, 138
C C R Nobbs, 110, 114, 116, 126, 135, 139, 172
C E Lane Poole, 160
Chamber of Commerce, 126
Charles Nobbs, 103
C H Currey, 59

Chilean Navy, 44
Christian Science Monitor, 185, 268
Christmas parcels, 152
Christopher Columbus, 38
Church of England Lands Ordinance 1937–1942, 108
Colonel A J Bennett, 122
Colonel Baird, 162
Colonel E T Leane, 98, 109, 111
Colonial Boundaries Act 1895, 26, 29, 82, 83, 97
Colonial Office, 15, 17, 18, 19, 20, 28, 29, 40, 43, 45, 58, 59, 72, 78, 80, 88, 92, 93, 94, 96, 170, 249, 254, 256
Committee of Returned Soldiers, 162
Commonwealth (Constitution section 123), 32
Commonwealth Electoral Act, 235, 238
Commonwealth Electoral Act 1918, 235
Commonwealth Government, 109, 122, 132, 133, 140, 149, 174, 181, 187, 200, 210, 213, 214, 216, 250
Commonwealth Grants Commission, 212
Commonwealth of Australia Constitution Act, 29, 80, 95, 244
Commonwealth Savings Bank of Australia, 170, 171
Commonwealth Trading Bank of Australia, 171
Commonwealth v. Yunupingu [2025] HCA 6, 246
Constitution section 121, 32
Cook Islands, 239
Cornelius Quintal, 116
Cottage Hospital, 172, 173
Councillor A B Commins, 177
Councillor A E Martin, 127
Councillor G G F Quintal, 177
Councillor Lesley Quintal, 131
Court of Petty Sessions, 158, 190
Crown Colony of Australia, 237
Crown Rents Ordinance 1934, 138
Customs, 17, 42, 104, 130, 177, 183, 184, 212, 222, 238, 243
Customs Ordinance 1934, 178
Customs Ordinance 1954, 178, 181, 184
Customs Ordinance 1955, 183

Customs Ordinance No. 7, 130, 131
Customs Ordinance No. 7 of 1934, 130
Cyrus, 43

D

Daily Telegraph, 161, 253, 254
Denmark, 145
Department of Defence, 148
Department of Lands, 169
Depression of the 1890s, 100
Devon, 151
Disjunction, 246
Docker report, 17
Dr A S Patton, 109
Dr Christopher Ward SC, 238
Dr Codrington, 76
Dr Gunn, 54
Dr L S Duke, 172
Dr Metcalfe, 6, 11
Dr Ward, 238
Ducie, 34
Duff, 42, 255, 256
Dutch East India Company, 39
Dutch New Guinea, 145

E

East Australia, 146
Eastern Coast of New South Wales, 64
Edmund Barton, 10, 77, 88
Education, 2, 43, 44, 47, 49, 182, 193, 213, 214, 222
Edward Quintal, 58
Edward Young, 36
Efate, 146
E G Whitlam, 202
Enlightenment, 40, 41, 61
E Stephenson, 172

Europe, 40, 42, 100, 101, 104, 145, 147, 161
Eustace Christian, 129
Executive Council Ordinance 1925, 128
Executive Council Ordinance 1925, Section 3(3), 128

F

F C Christian, 191
F C Urquhart, 109
Federal Attorney-General's Department, 30, 83
Federal compact, 244, 245
Ferny Lane and Pine Avenue, 150
Fiji, 88, 146, 250, 268
Finlay and Carson, 29, 79
First Proviso to Section 5, 65
First Schedule of No. 40 of 1936, 136
Fishing, 108, 211, 222
F J Needham, 179, 185
F J Tattle, 162
Fletcher Christian, 35, 36
F M Bladen, 117
France, 38, 40, 101, 144
Francis Whysall, 110
Franklin Bates, 171
Frankyn C Christian, 176
F R M Crozier, 162
F W Pearson, 171

G

Gaudron J, 243, 245, 247
General Assembly, 239
General Douglas MacArthur, 146
General Sir Archibald Wavell, 145
George Hunn Nobbs, 43, 44, 49, 58, 251, 259
George Reid, 20
Germany, 99, 100, 101, 144, 145, 147, 152, 161
GMV *Maui Pomare*, 123

Government of Norfolk Island, 25, 65, 81, 82, 92, 194, 269
Governor Bourke, 64, 261
Governor General Denison, 219
Governor-General of the Commonwealth of Australia in Canberra, 129
Governor Lord Loftus, 75
Governor of New South Wales, 12, 20, 25, 28, 31, 45, 60, 62, 64, 67, 68, 72, 77, 78, 79, 86, 88, 89, 92, 93, 256
Governor of Norfolk Island, 12, 24, 76, 78, 93, 169, 256
Great Depression, 99, 123, 141
Greg Quintal, 198

H

Havannah Harbour, 146
Hawkesworth's Voyages in 1773, 34
Health services of Norfolk Island, 233
Henderson, 34, 43
Henry Menges, 102, 104, 112, 116
Henry Wilkinson, 75, 267
Hercules, 43
High Court of Australia, 4, 137, 156, 221
HMAV *Bounty*, 35, 36
HMS *Basilisk*, 55
HMS *Briton*, 37
HMS *Calypso*, 55
HMS *Challenger*, 45
HMS *Comet*, 45
HMS *Curacoa*, 54
HMS *Daphne*, 56
HMS *Fly*, 38
HMS *Herald*, 62
HMS *Juno*, 59
HM Sloop *Fly*, 68
HMS *Pandora*, 35, 55
HMS *Sparrowhawk*, 54
HMS *Spy*, 55
HMS *Tagus*, 37

HMS *Talbot*, 54
HMS *Virago*, 58
Holland, 26, 39, 145
Holland (Dutch), 145
Holmes, 223
Honourable J H Carruthers MLA, 21
Honourable Paul Hasluck, 175
Honourable R J Ellicott QC, 217
House of Representatives Standing Committee, 232, 233
H S Edgar JP, 102
H S Newberry, 179
Human Rights and Equal Opportunity Commission, 232

I

Ilyk, 223
Immigration, 212, 222, 228, 234, 238
Immigration Ordinance, 215
Imperial Act 6 & 7 Vic c35, 30
Imperial Act 18 and 19 Vict. Cap. 56, 93
India, 38, 39
Indian Ocean, 38, 146
Inquiry into Governance on Norfolk Island, 233, 236
Inquiry into Norfolk Island electoral matters, 233
Internal territories, 244, 245, 246
International Court of Justice, 238
In the pink or in the red, 233
Isaac Martin, 36
Isaac Newton, 41

J

J A Carrodus, 102
Jakarta, 39
James Morrison, 36
Japan, 39, 145, 146, 147, 152
J D Patterson, 191
J F C Quintal, 191
J H Catts, 104, 106

John Adams, 36, 37, 44
John Buffett, 43, 55
John Cole, 16
John Evans, 43, 44
John Mills, 36
John Watkins, 87
John Williams, 36
Joint Standing Committee, 233, 236
Joshua Hill, 45, 46
J R Halligan of the Prime Minister's Department, Canberra, 132
Judge Docker, 16, 77
Judiciary Ordinance 1936, 136, 153, 156
Judy Marty, 237
J Westwood, 179

K

Kingston, 138, 140, 164, 173, 174, 193, 206

L

Labor Prime Minister John Curtin, 145
Ladies' Auxiliary Committee, 172
Lady Rosenthal, 139
Law Reform Commission, 217
L D Holloway, 191
Legislative Drafting Division, 213
Letters Patent dated 24 October 1843, 30
Licensing of Boats Ordinance 1934, No 14, 131
Lieutenant Colonel A R Cockerell, DSO, 151
Lieutenant Colonel J W Barry, 151
Lighterage Ordinance 1961 (No. 6), 131
Liquor Ordinance of 1960, 206
London Missionary Society, 41, 43, 251, 254, 258, 259
Lord Chelmsford, 92, 94
Lord Howe Island, 26, 75, 102
L V Nola, 191

M

Magistrates, 71, 113, 114, 136, 158, 217
Magistrates Court of the Australian Capital Territory, 158
Major General R H Wordsworth, 200
Major General V C M Sellheim, 121, 172
Malaya, 145
Malay Peninsula, 145
Māori, 50
Mason J, 242, 245
Matthew McCoy, 59
Matthew Quintal, 36
McCasker, 223
McIntyre, 223, 251, 258, 262, 265
McKenzie, 223
Melanesian Mission, 76, 98, 108, 118, 141, 143, 150, 173, 267
Melanesian Mission Trust Board, 173
Messrs Catts, West, Matthews, Anstey, W Johnston, Piggot, and Palmer, 102
Metcalfe, 6, 7, 9, 11
M H McLelland QC, 237
Michael V Murphy, 99
Middle East, 39, 145
Middlegate, 163, 174
Migration Act 1958 (Cth), 234
Minister for Territories, 133, 178
Minister Jim Lloyd, 236
Miriam Christian, 62, 68
Miss Gordina Nobbs, 172
Mission Estate, 171
M L Treadgold, 158, 262, 265, 266
Morayshire, 61, 68
Mount Pitt, 138
Mr A B Keith, 94
Mr Batchelor, 96
Mr Chamberlain, 19
Mr Charles Oliver, 21

Mr D V O'Leary, 223
Mr Ellicott, 218, 221, 237
Mr Fisher, 92, 93, 94, 96
Mr G Adams, 7
Mr Groom, 91
Mr Harcourt, 96
Mr Houston, 87
Mr Isaacs, Attorney-General, 33
Mr Justice C E Herbert, 121
Mr Lowe, 238
Mr Macarthur-Onslow, 132
Mr Meade, 15, 256
Mr Neville, 240
Mrs Gordina Beveridge, 172, 176
Mrs Kathleen Walsh, 176
Mrs Kelly, 240
Mrs Kit Donkin, 191
Mr Thompson, 240
Mt Pitt reserve area, 223
Murphy J, 242
Mutiny Descendants Stir, 185

N

N C Christian, 191
Needham, 179, 185, 191, 198, 199, 203
Netherlands East Indies, 145, 146
Newbold, 191
New Caledonia, 146, 149
New Guinea, 32, 84, 145, 146, 198, 200
New Hebrides, 146, 170
New South Wales, 10, 12, 15, 17, 18, 19, 20, 21, 22, 23, 24,
    25, 26, 28, 29, 30, 31, 45, 60, 62, 63, 64, 66, 67, 68, 71,
    72, 73, 74, 75, 76, 77, 78, 79, 81, 85, 86, 88, 89, 91, 92,
    93, 95, 96, 97, 118, 149, 157, 169, 215, 220, 238, 249,
    250, 251, 253, 255, 256
New South Wales Department of Education, 215
New Zealand, 23, 50, 69, 78, 88, 93, 94, 96, 98, 101, 123, 124,

284   Index

    125, 139, 141, 142, 146, 147, 148, 149, 151, 152, 159,
    161, 175, 206, 239, 250, 260, 265
New Zealand Division of the Royal Navy, 148
N Force, 151, 152
Nicolaus Copernicus, 41
Nimmo Commission, 218
Nimmo report, 218, 219, 270
Noah Bunker, 44
Norfolk Island, 3, 4, 6, 8, 9, 10, 11, 12, 13, 18, 19, 20, 23, 24,
    25, 26, 27, 28, 29, 30, 31, 43, 45, 53, 57, 58, 59, 60, 61,
    62, 63, 64, 65, 66, 67, 68, 69, 70, 71, 72, 73, 74, 75, 76,
    77, 78, 79, 80, 81, 82, 83, 84, 85, 86, 87, 88, 89, 90, 91,
    92, 93, 94, 95, 96, 97, 98, 99, 101, 102, 103, 106, 107,
    108, 109, 110, 111, 112, 113, 116, 117, 121, 124, 126,
    129, 130, 131, 132, 133, 134, 135, 136, 139, 140, 142,
    147, 148, 149, 150, 151, 152, 153, 154, 155, 156, 157,
    158, 160, 161, 162, 163, 164, 166, 167, 168, 169, 170,
    171, 173, 174, 175, 176, 178, 179, 180, 181, 182, 184,
    185, 187, 188, 189, 190, 191, 192, 193, 194, 200, 201,
    202, 203, 207, 209, 210, 211, 213, 214, 215, 216, 217,
    218, 219, 220, 221, 222, 223, 224, 225, 232, 233, 234,
    235, 236, 237, 238, 239, 240, 241, 242, 243, 245, 246,
    247, 248, 249, 250, 251, 252, 253, 254, 255, 256, 257,
    258, 259, 260, 262, 263, 266, 267, 268, 269, 270
Norfolk Island Act 1913, 27, 84, 86, 99, 134, 169, 170, 188
Norfolk Island Act 1957, 184, 185, 187, 188, 190, 217, 268
Norfolk Island Act 1979, 217, 225, 232, 233, 234, 235
Norfolk Island Act (No. 101 of 1963), 202
Norfolk Island Amendment Act 2004, 241, 242
Norfolk Island Amendment Bill 1999, 233
Norfolk Island Association, 130, 131, 155, 266
Norfolk Island Bill 1913, 28, 97
Norfolk Island Bill 1963, 202
Norfolk Island Bill 1978, 217
Norfolk Island Boating Company, 130, 131
Norfolk Island Citizens' Progress Association, 179, 184
Norfolk Island Cooperative Dairy Co Ltd, 140

Norfolk Island Council Ordinance 1960, 188, 190, 192
Norfolk Island Court of Petty Sessions, 158
Norfolk Island Executive Council, 232, 252
Norfolk Island Government, 131, 189, 236, 252
Norfolk Island Government Gazette, 131, 189
Norfolk Island Hospital Board, 173, 174, 267
Norfolk Island Infantry Detachment, 148, 162
Norfolk Island Legislation Amendment Act 2015 (Cth), 238
Norfolk Island Legislative Assembly, 222, 232, 234, 235
Norfolk Island Lighterage Service, 131
Norfolk Island Ordinance 1964, 202
Norfolk Island Penny Savings Bank, 171
Norfolk Island Penny Savings Bank Ordinance 1935, 171
Norfolk Island Progress Association, 112, 184, 268
Norfolk Island Public Hospital Ordinance 1953, 175
Norfolk Island's *Immigration Act* and human rights, 232
Norfolk Island Territory Assembly, 211
Norfolk Island Volunteer Reserve, 162
Norfolk Island Weekly, 161, 163, 164, 166, 167, 253, 266
Norfolk News in 1958, 163, 169
Northern Territory, 109, 198, 200, 231, 244, 247
Northern Territory of South Australia, 244
Northern Territory (Self-Government) Regulations 1978 (Regulation 4), 231
Norway, 145
Nunn, 223

O

Oceania, 39, 42
Oeno, 34
On legal and constitutional affairs, 232
On the National Capital and External Territories, 233, 236
Order in Council, 12, 20, 23, 24, 25, 26, 27, 28, 29, 30, 31, 32, 65, 66, 67, 68, 71, 74, 78, 79, 80, 81, 82, 83, 84, 85, 91, 93, 97, 261
Order-in-Council of 15 January 1897, 29
Order in Council of 18 October 1900, 27

Order of Her Majesty in Council, 60, 72
Ordinance No. 4 of 1934, 128
Ordinance No. 7, 130, 131, 132
Ordinance No. 10 of 1935, 134
Ordinance No. 14 of 1934, 131
Ordinance Revision Ordinance 1964, 169
Original States, 243, 244

P

Pacific Cable, 88, 91, 252
Pacific Fisheries and Trading Company, 106, 107
Pacific Ocean area, 146, 147
Palestine, 145
Papua Act 1905, 33, 84, 86, 95
Papua Bill, 32, 84
Passenger Movement Charge Amendment (Norfolk Island) Act 2016, 238
Pearl Harbor, 145, 147
Peru, 44
Peter Heywood, 36
Philippines, 145, 146
Phoney war, 144, 145
Pitcairners, 8, 10, 18, 57, 59, 60, 61, 109, 116, 122, 156, 171, 218, 251, 257
Pitcairn Island, 3, 4, 11, 21, 34, 36, 37, 38, 40, 42, 43, 44, 52, 54, 57, 58, 68, 69, 70, 225, 257, 259
Pitcairn Island Fund, 21, 57, 58
Pitcairn Island Register, 54, 259
Pitcairn's Island and the Islanders, 52, 68, 249, 258
Planters Association, 126
P L Ryan, 195
Polynesian, 35, 36
Portugal, 38, 39
Post Office, 170, 171, 193
Preamble, 224
Prime Minister Menzies, 144

Prime Minister's Department, 130, 132, 148, 167
PRIMISTER, 166
Prince Consort, 58
Printers and Newspapers Ordinance 1935–1936, 168, 169
Professor Crawford AC SC FBA, 237

Q

Qantas, 216
Queen Victoria, 58, 64, 66, 218
Quintal, 36, 58, 68, 116, 131, 171, 177, 191, 198, 223
Quis Custodiet Ipsos Custodes?, 233, 236

R

Racial Discrimination Act 1975, 216
Recruiting March in Sydney, 162
Referendum, 223, 238
Report of House of Representatives Standing Committee on transport and regional services, 233
Report of inquiry into Norfolk Island electoral matters, 233
Report of inquiry into regional aviation services in Australia, 233
Report of Joint Standing Committee on the National Capital and External Territories (JSCNCET), 233
Report of the Senate Standing Committee on legal and constitutional legislation, 233
Reuben Denison, 62, 68
R H H Nobbs, 178, 191
Right Honourable Henry Labouchere, 60
Right Honourable Sir George Pearce KCVO, 132
R J Rain, 150, 265
RMS *Strathaird*, 125
Robert Pitcairn, 34
Royal Australian Navy, 148
Royal Navy, 144, 148
Royal New Zealand Air Force, 152, 175
Russel Ward, 144
R Westlake, 196

S

Samoa, 146
Sandwich Islands, 55
Sapientissimuss, 207
Schedules 2 and 3 to the Act, 226
Scientific Revolution, 40, 41
Scolypopa australis, 159
Second imperial force, 144, 145, 149
Section 5 of 18 and 19 Vict, c.56, 79
Section 51, 242, 246
Section 90, 242, 244
Section 121, 243
Section 122, 95, 243
Section 122 of the Constitution, 27, 28, 29, 80, 81, 84, 89, 91, 92, 237, 241, 246
Section 123 of the Constitution, 32, 241, 244
Sections 123 and 124, 243
Select Committee on the Republic Referendum, 237
Self-government, 5, 132, 183, 197, 219, 221, 222, 225, 233, 239
Senate Hansard for 3 March 2004, 240
Senate Hansard for December 2003, 240
Senator Despoja, 240
Senator Hill, 240
Senator Hogg, 240
Senator Humphries, 240
Senator Lightfoot, 240
Senator O'Brien, 240
Senators McDougall and Blakey, 102
Senator the Honourable R G Withers, 217
Senator Withers, 218, 221
S E Nobbs, 191
Singapore, 146
Sir Arthur Fadden, 178
Sir Charles Rosenthal, 139
Sir C Lucas, 94, 96

Sir Harry Rawson, 86, 87
Sir John Angus Nimmo CBE, 209
Sir John Barrow, 45
Sir John Young, 14
Sir Joseph Ward, 94
Sir Robert Garran, 28, 30, 83, 84, 86
Sir Thomas Staines, 37
Sir William Denison, 10, 59, 60, 72, 261
S Leydin, 192
Snell, 223
Society for Promoting Christian Knowledge, 43, 56, 58, 251, 253, 254, 258, 259
Solomon Islands, 108, 146, 149
South China Sea, 146
South Pacific Command, 148, 149, 151
South Pacific Commission, 185, 268
South Pacific Ocean, 34, 35
Special Committee, 239
SS *Morinda*, 124, 125, 130
Statute 6 and 7 Vic c.35, 64, 85
Stephen Christian, 10
Subsection 19(1) of the Act, 225
Sumatra, 146
Supreme Court, 190, 217, 238
Supreme Court Judges, 217
Svikart v. Stewart [1994] 125 ALR 534, 246
Sydney, Australia, 34
Sydney Morning Herald, 105, 253, 254
Syrette, 223

T

Tahiti, 35, 36, 37, 42, 45, 56, 59
Tahitians, 42
Tasmania, 12, 71, 169
T Bailey, 179
Territories Legislation Amendment Act 2016 (Cth), 238
Territory of the Commonwealth of Australia, 210

The Calcutta Journal, 43
The War Day by Day, 162
Thomas Buffett, 58
Timor, 36, 240
Timor-Leste v. Australia, 240
Tom C Lee, 176
Tonga, 146
Topaz, 37
Torres Strait, 36
Tourist Bureau, 126
Tree of Knowledge, 163
Tubuai, 35

U

United Nations Association of Australia, 218
United Nations General Assembly Resolution 1514 of 14 December 1960, 239
United States, 145, 146, 147, 185, 251
United States Asiatic Fleet, 145
United States Navy, 146

V

Valparaíso, 34, 54, 55, 56
Van Diemen's Land, 30, 31, 60, 64, 65, 66, 71, 72, 73, 85
Vaughan Lowe KC, 238, 240
Vice Admiral H F Leary, 146
Vice Admiral R L Ghormley, 147
Vice Admiral Sir Fairfax Moresby, 57, 68
Viscount Hampden, 19
Volunteer Motor Transport Corps, 162

W

Walleys, 35
Walter Brodie, 52, 68, 258, 260
War Precautions Act 1914, 100
Webster and Finlay, 28, 78

Wellington West Coast Regiment, 151
W H Scott, 194
William Brown, 36
William McCoy, 36
William McLachlan, 176
W McLachlan, 153
W M Randall, 191, 198
W N Selby Newbald, 177, 180
W N S Newbald, 179
World War I, 98, 100, 101, 108, 141
World War II, 3, 98, 144, 161, 250, 265
W Quintal, 171
W Simmonds, 179
W T McCoy, 191

Y

Yarmouth, England, 44
Yaron Finkelstein, 237

ABOUT THE AUTHOR

Don Wright is a lawyer with a deep knowledge and love for Norfolk Island. Accepting a position as Legal Advisor in 1983, Don held several senior positions in the territory's Administration and Government in the nine years he lived there. At one of the highest levels, he represented Norfolk Island in the Bennett v. Commonwealth case to change constitutional law.

Don grew to love Norfolk Island. He found it intellectually rewarding and discovered a tight-knit community which embraced him and his family. Don's first child was born on the island and his wife established a family-run restaurant called 'Moira' there. Don even learnt to fly small planes during his time in the territory.

Before Norfolk, Don was the Assistant Editor of the New Zealand Law Reports, and after leaving Norfolk, Don was a Commercial Litigation Partner in a Sydney law firm. Since his university days in Wellington, Don has continued his study and love of philosophy and now reads it for leisure.

Today, Don spends most of his time writing in his Sydney home.

www.ingramcontent.com/pod-product-compliance
Lightning Source LLC
Chambersburg PA
CBHW020358080526
44584CB00014B/1072